GROWING UP IN RIVER CITY

GROWING

RIVER

COMMITTEE ON HUMAN DEVELOPMENT

THE UNIVERSITY OF CHICAGO

NEW YORK   LONDON

UP IN

CITY

ROBERT J. HAVIGHURST

PAUL HOOVER BOWMAN

GORDON P. LIDDLE

CHARLES V. MATTHEWS

JAMES V. PIERCE

JOHN WILEY AND SONS, INC.

Library of Congress Catalog Card Number: 62-17461
Printed in the United States of America

TO FABIOLA C. MOORMAN

PREFACE

THIS IS an account of the growing up of an age group in "River City," a Midwestern city of 45,000. It presents the results of a research study carried on by a group of social scientists from the University of Chicago during the years 1951 to 1960. The children in this study are a control group for an action-research program designed to help a community do a better job of rearing its children. The results of that experiment will be reported at a later time.

The members of the group treated in this book were all in the sixth grade of school when the study commenced, and most of them were 11 years old. When the study closed most of them were 20 years old. Those who went to college were, for the most part, in their second year. Those who graduated from high school and went to work had time enough to settle into a way of adult life. More than half of the girls were married. Thus the study carries this age group from childhood into early adulthood.

The method used in this study was that of observing a group of children in their natural habitat as they grew up. They were studied as they studied, played, and worked in the schools, churches, homes, and shops of the community.

For this kind of study the fullest cooperation is needed from the schools, youth-serving agencies, churches, employers, police, and welfare agencies. This kind of cooperation and assistance was enjoyed, largely because the research was conducted under the auspices of the Community Youth Development Commission, an organization consisting of representatives of some 25 youth-serving organizations in the community. The Commission shares responsibility with the University of Chicago for the research. All major publications of the research staff are read and approved by the Commission before they are published. The research staff, in addition to being employees of the University, are residents of the community and participate in the life of its schools, churches, and other organizations.

Under the auspices of the Youth Development Commission a Professional Committee was formed of professional workers with youth from the various youth-serving organizations. This committee facilitates cooperation among these organizations and has been of great assistance in the conduct of this particular research.

The principal purpose of this book is to show in what way the social backgrounds and personal characteristics of boys and girls determine how well they perform their tasks of growing up in this kind of community. For that reason there is a theme of prediction running through the study. The question is asked and answered, again and again: "Knowing these facts about boys and girls in the sixth grade, or in the ninth grade, what can we predict about their performance in the later years of high school, or after they graduate from high school?" Then a further question is asked: "Under what conditions do boys and girls grow into competent young adults, and under what conditions do they become incompetent young adults?"

Comparisons of this study with *Elmtown's Youth*, by A. B. Hollingshead, are inevitable. Both studies have been made under the auspices of the Committee on Human Development, and in the same part of the country. This study has a longitudinal dimension, however, that is lacking in *Elmtown's Youth*, and employs a program of testing of various sorts, extending from the sixth to the twelfth grade. *Elmtown's Youth* rested primarily upon an extraordinarily skilful and talented interview procedure which permitted the teen-agers of that community to tell about their communal life with great frankness and liveliness. *Elmtown's Youth* deals with a wider range of the social aspects of adolescent life, stressing such topics as social cliques and dating, recreation, church differences, and gives a graphic picture of high-school life, whereas this book is focused more on movement from childhood through adolescence to adulthood.

Both studies see social class as a basic and determining characteristic in the lives of boys and girls. However, there are major differences in the way this concept is used. *Elmtown's Youth* was a product of what may be called the "muck-raking period" of social-class analysis. The concept was a novel one to American readers; it had the quality of startling and even shocking people; it made them sit up and take notice. Coming during the depression of the 1930's and shortly afterward, these early studies of social class expressed some of the then current questioning and discontent with the social structure of the United States. The present senior author was one of those who made the earlier studies, and has observed a change in his own attitudes toward social-class analysis with the passage of time.

The difference between *Elmtown's Youth* and *Growing Up in River City* is partly one of temporal change. *Elmtown's Youth* reports the life of teen-agers in 1942–1943, a full 15 years earlier than the time described in River City. *Elmtown's Youth* came at a time when the Great Depression was still a grim memory, and the youth of Elmtown grew up during the Depression. The youth of River City grew up during the post-war economic boom, a time of full employment and unparalleled prosperity.

Social class can be seen in either of two ways. It may be regarded as the villain causing conflict and disharmony in society. On the other hand, it may be seen as an inevitable part of social structure. Social classes can be seen as working harmoniously together to get the business of society accomplished and to give some order and stability to social life. Instead of seeing nothing but class warfare in society, it is possible to see with a substantial degree of truth a cooperation of social classes. The working class needs the middle class, and vice versa. Youth from working class homes can choose between the rewards of upward social mobility, which are open to many of them, and the rewards of a stable working-class life with a rising standard of living. Middle-class youth have to work hard to avoid downward mobility. Democracy consists of maintaining a fluid society with movement up and down in the society based upon effort and ability. To a considerable extent River City illustrates this sort of democracy, and this book reports it.

Thus, as we observe the growing up of a post-war generation in River City, we try to present a realistic account of the process as a basis for thinking about educational and social policies.

Robert J. Havighurst

Chicago, Illinois
May, 1962

ACKNOWLEDGMENTS

To the citizens of River City, and to the boys and girls and their families, we express our gratitude and appreciation. We have tried to report accurately on our careful study of the process of growing up. We hope that this work will contribute to better living for boys and girls in this and other communities. This book will be read with special interest by those living in our experimental community, and it is inevitable that attempts will be made to identify the persons about whom case reports are given. May we clearly state that we have disguised the names and descriptions of people to such an extent that all persons presented in the book are fictitious. Consequently no person can be identified in these pages, and no one's privacy has been invaded.

In view of the fact that we are not calling River City by its real name, we cannot readily acknowledge by name the individuals who were most helpful in the work of the research. However, there are certain groups of people whose assistance should be recognized. The school principals and teachers have been most willing to give the benefit of their unique knowledge of the children. The pastors of the various churches and the employers for whom the young people have worked have responded readily to our questions. The members of the Community Youth Development Commission, who have guided the work of the project, have given their time to meetings with the research staff, and have helped at the places where local community leadership was essential.

Certain individuals have been especially important in the research work, and they can be mentioned by the roles which they fill. The secretary of the Youth Development Commission has been a most important person in the operation of the project, serving as a liaison officer between research specialists and the community agencies, and also contributing substantially to the research through her own experience and knowledge of the community.

The superintendent of schools has been a generous and wise supporter of the project, always willing to use his influence in the interest of doing a better job for the youth of the community. The principals of the junior and senior high schools have made data available through their office staffs, and have given the research staff the benefit of their wisdom and experience in the conduct of the research.

The director of special education has served as liaison officer between the schools and the research staff, making arrangements for the collection of data, and using his influence and knowledge to clear up many important details of research operations. The assistant superintendent of schools has been a wise counselor and a force for improvement in the schools in the experimental aspects of the research project.

Especially valuable as a source of information has been a junior high school counselor who has given his summers to interviewing for the project, and has proven to be a "born" interviewer. Most of the interviews with parents and with dropout students were made by him. The police chief, the police matron, and the county judge, and their staffs have been willing and helpful sources of information. The executive officers of the agencies which serve youth and their families have formed a Professional Committee which has met with members of the research staff and they have been of great assistance, individually and as a group, in the design and conduct of the research.

'MRS. FABIOLA C. MOORMAN has given more help than any other single person, in many important areas. Not only has she been interested in the financing of the study, through the C. A. Moorman Foundation; but also has taken a warm personal interest in this study and has served faithfully on the Youth Development Commission. Her interests in the betterment of community life and in mental health have given her a basis for being constructive and supportive in her advice. At the same time she has scrupulously avoided any possible interference in the technical work of the project. The research staff members all feel grateful for the interest shown by Fabiola Moorman in them and their families as well as in the work of the project. Her dedication to people, and particularly to the people of this community, has helped the staff to keep its work in perspective.

CONTENTS

CHILDHOOD

I

~~~~

THE CHILDREN AND THE COMMUNITY

THIS BOOK tells how a cohort of children grew up through adolescence in the medium-sized mid-western community of River City. The story commences with the children in the sixth grade of the public schools, most of them 11 years old, and ends nine years later when, as 20-year-olds, they were all through school and some had finished a year of college.

When the story starts the children had already been molded by family and school influences into persons with a past and a fairly predictable future.

A considerable part of the book deals with predictions that were made and the extent to which these predictions came true. Questions such as the following are answered:

Which ones turned out very well?
Which ones became delinquent?
Which ones did very well in school?
Which ones went to college?
Which ones dropped out of school?
Which ones married early?

The children were studied in the sixth grade and predictions were made about their success or failure in school and their social and emotional development.

3

The chief formative influences working upon these boys and girls were studied. Emphasis was mainly laid on the family and the school, with somewhat less attention to the church and the youth-serving organizations such as Scouts and the YMCA and YWCA.

Growing up to age 20 consists for this cohort of children in going to school, finishing or dropping out of high school, getting part-time or full-time jobs, going to college, and getting married. Hence these matters were recorded and are reported and analyzed.

This particular group was merely studied and its growth recorded as part of a broad project, as yet not completed, in which a younger cohort was being helped as much as possible. This present group was a control group, whose history was to be left undisturbed for comparison with the experimental group.

Consequently, the story of the growth of this cohort is a common story of what happened in the decade of the 1950's in medium-sized communities in the central part of the United States.

THE CHILDREN

The subjects of this study were all of the boys and girls in the sixth grade of the River City public schools in 1951–1952, with the addition of those who joined this cohort in the following three years, those sixth graders who attended a Lutheran parochial school and a small, private boarding school for boys, and those in special classes (physically handicapped, mentally retarded, sight-saving) of similar grade level. This last group was included to get the full range of mental ability found in a school population. The children of the mentally handicapped group were all born in the year 1939, one year ahead of most of the regular sixth-grade group. This choice was made to have as homogenous a social group as possible. Members of the mentally handicapped group tend to be somewhat retarded socially, and it was decided that those born in the year 1939 would be a more "natural" subgroup of the total than would those born a year earlier or a year later.

Pupils in the Roman Catholic parochial schools were not studied because arrangements could not be made for the research staff to work in those schools. Some 32 per cent of elementary school children in River City were in the Roman Catholic parochial schools.

There were about 400 children in the sixth-grade group defined in 1951. In the seventh and eighth grades a normal amount of moving in and out of the community added 31 to the number of names on the roster. Then, in the ninth grade there was an influx of 67 from the parochial elementary schools and from the rural elementary schools at the fringes of the city. When the roll was closed, in 1955, there were 487 names, almost evenly divided between boys and girls. The birth years of the children are shown in Table 1.

TABLE 1. BIRTH YEARS OF THE STUDY GROUP

Year of Birth	Boys	Girls
1937	3	2
1938	16	8
1939	64	50
1940	159	178
1941	5	1
1943	0	1
Total	247	240

THE STRUCTURE OF THIS BOOK

This book is like a house with a foundation and three storeys, as is illustrated in the "Scheme of the Book." For a foundation there is an account of the community and the institutions that orient the child—family, social class, and youth-serving organizations. The child is equipped for growth by these institutions with a personality and a set of abilities. The first four chapters describe these foundations on which the child's life is built.

Next comes the growth of the child through middle childhood and early adolescence. This is centered in the school, where the child does well or poorly pretty much in relation to his equipment of personality and abilities. The church supplements the school but not for all children, as seen in Chapter 7. Failure in school leads a number of boys to the dead end of delinquency, as demonstrated in Chapter 6, although some boys are able to outgrow school failure and to do fairly well as workers in the next stage of growth.

After secondary school the pathway of growth divides into three: college for some, work for the majority, and marriage for many of the girls. These paths in their turn, lead into young adulthood.

SCHEME OF THE BOOK

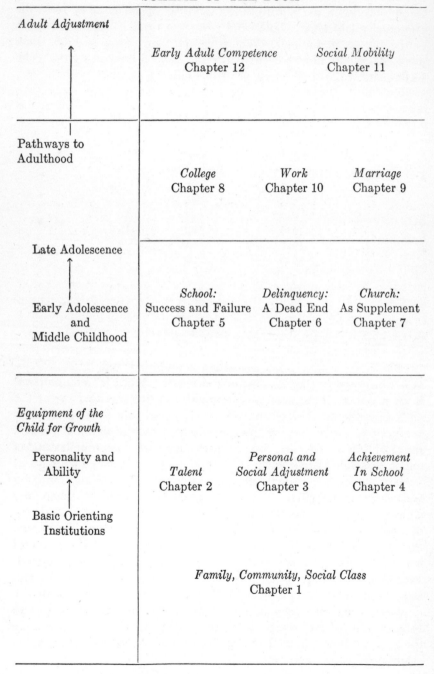

Adult Adjustment

Early Adult Competence   Social Mobility
Chapter 12   Chapter 11

Pathways to
Adulthood

College   Work   Marriage
Chapter 8   Chapter 10   Chapter 9

Late Adolescence

Early Adolescence
and
Middle Childhood

School: Delinquency: Church:
Success and Failure A Dead End   As Supplement
Chapter 5   Chapter 6   Chapter 7

*Equipment of the
Child for Growth*

Personality and
Ability

Talent   Personal and   Achievement
           Social Adjustment   In School
Chapter 2 Chapter 3   Chapter 4

Basic Orienting
Institutions

Family, Community, Social Class
Chapter 1

Knowing the equipment of a boy or girl for growth, it is possible to predict how he will turn out. Furthermore, on the basis of experience with these predictions it should be possible to point out where the most can be gained by improving the institutions that serve the child—schools, churches and youth-serving agencies of various kinds. This is the plan to be followed in this book: making predictions of the success of young people on the basis of earlier information about them, and pointing out where some of their failure might have been avoided.

THE COMMUNITY

River City, county seat of Van Buren County, has approximately 44,000 residents in a county population of 65,000. River City was founded in the 1820 decade by settlers from New England and New York. Its period of most rapid growth was 1840 to 1870. Then followed a slow growth to 1900, when River City had a population of 36,000 and Van Buren County had 67,000, more than it has today. River City is the largest center of population within a radius of 60 miles. It is independent, not a satellite of a metropolis.

More than half of the labor force in the county is industrial, but there is a substantial rural population, making this a typical Midwestern county. There is no one predominant industry, but a number of industrial concerns make a wide variety of products.

Located on the Great Inland River, the city had a substantial river trade in the last century and still bears some of the traditional characteristics of a river town. River City has a strong cultural tradition, and it is known particularly as a community that appreciates good music.

The city is a product of two major cultural streams. Beginning as an outpost of settlers from New England and New York, it attracted large numbers of German immigrants in the middle of the nineteenth century. These people settled in one half of the growing city. They bought deep narrow lots on which they built small houses near the street and a barn on the rear alley. Many of them kept a family cow, and these animals with their calves wandered at will grazing on the open lots. This section of the city came to be known as "Calftown." There were further German immigrants after World War I, and there has been very little immigration from Eastern or Southern Europe.

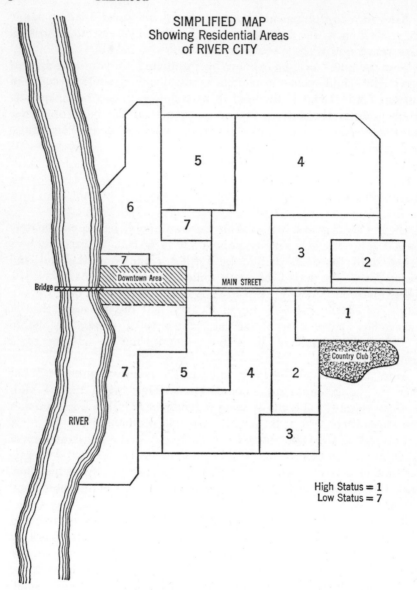

SIMPLIFIED MAP
Showing Residential Areas
of RIVER CITY

5

4

6

7

7

Downtown Area

Bridge   MAIN STREET

3

2

1

7

5

4

2

Country Club

3

RIVER

High Status = 1
Low Status = 7

A third cultural stream came in from the rural border states, old Americans with a "hillbilly" background. They and their descendents form much of the lower socio-economic stratum today.

Negroes make up about 3 per cent of the population, and have been stable in numbers for several generations. There has not been much overt racial friction, and Negro children attend school with white children in the nearest school building. But economic opportunities are not very good for them, and consequently the Negro children who finish high school are likely to go to larger cities in search of better vocational opportunity.

River City believes that it is more conservative than some of its sister communities in the Midwest, a matter of pride to some and of discontent to others. In any case, it is a pleasant city to see, especially in the spring and the autumn. It occupies a lordly site upon the bluffs overlooking the river, and has several fine residential streets with large mansions built about 1900 and set in expansive tree-shaded lawns. Most people in River City believe that it is a "good place in which to live and bring up children."

THE SOCIAL STRUCTURE

In this book we will not trouble to demonstrate the well-known fact that there is a heirarchy of social-economic status in a community like River City. We will take this for granted and proceed to study the several observable social classes as they affect the development of children.

There are four clearly differentiated social classes in River City. Each class provides a social environment for its children that differs importantly from the environments provided by the other classes. It is important to describe these social environments, for the fact of social class membership will be one of the principal items to which the development of boys and girls in River City will be related.

The method used to study and describe the social structure of River City has been developed by Warner and his collaborators in a number of community studies. This method was adapted to River City as soon as it became clear through preliminary study that this community had a basic similarity to the others that had already been investigated in the Middle West.

The socio-economic status of each child in the study group was determined by means of the Index of Status Characteristics (ISC), which is described in the Appendix. For each child there is an ISC score. In addition, each child was identified as belonging to one of the following socio-economic groups:

Upper or upper-middle class   Group A
Lower-middle class   Group B
Upper-lower class   Group C
Lower-lower class   Group D

Table 2 shows how the study group members are distributed among the four social-class subgroups.

TABLE 2. SOCIAL CLASS DISTRIBUTION
(PERCENTAGE DISTRIBUTION)

Social Class	Male	Female
A (Upper and upper-middle)	9	9
B (Lower-middle)	26	27
C (Upper-lower)	37	40
D (Lower-lower)	28	24
Number	247	240

The Four Social-Class Groups

The highest social-class group recognized for the purposes of this study is really a combination of what are generally known as the upper and upper-middle classes. There are so few children of upper-class families that they cannot usefully be studied as a group. They associate freely with upper-middle class children. Accordingly, Class A is a mixture.

Class A—Upper and Upper-Middle Classes. Class A extends from the very top of the prestige structure in River City almost to the bottom of the professional and managerial groups. Boys and girls in this group attend the local public or parochial schools as a matter of course, but a few of the high-status families send their children away to a private preparatory school for the last year or two of high school. In this study group, only 4 of 43 Class A children went away to preparatory schools.

The family incomes of this group range upward from as low as seven or eight thousand dollars in 1959 value. They live in the better homes of the old residential sections or in the new ranch-house style dwellings in the Country Club area. The parents generally have had at least some college education, and they almost universally expect their children to enter college.

These people are the community leaders in social as well as in business and professional life. The children observe their parents in positions of leadership and get the feeling that they themselves have a leadership obligation in the school and in youth groups.

Class B—Lower-Middle Class. Class B consists of the people with minor "white collar" jobs plus a few highly skilled manual workers. Their children make up 26 per cent of the study population, and through numbers gain the large part of the positions of leadership and recognition in the adolescent world of the school and community, even though a higher proportion of the small number of Class A members attain such positions.

The lower-middle class live a comfortable life in River City. Their jobs and incomes are stable. For the most part they own their own homes in middle residential districts. They are able to give their children whatever material advantages they need, and even to help them with college expenses.

Though very few adults of Class B have gone to college, they are increasingly expecting their children to go to college, and the absolute number of college entrants from this group now exceeds the number from Class A. College is recognized as important as a means of upward social mobility for the children of Class B.

From Class B comes the numerical support for most church and charitable activities and associations.

Class C—Upper-Lower Class. Class C is the largest group in River City. It consists of respectable, hard-working manual workers and an occasional proprietor of a small business that does not require more than a few hundred dollars of investment.

Since the close of the Second World War Class C members have had steady employment. Nearly all of them own automobiles, and many own their own small homes which are located mainly in the areas rated 4, 5, and 6 on the map.

The parents in this class have had relatively less schooling than those in classes A and B. Some of them have graduated from high school, and most of them have completed elementary school. They are interested in the education of their children, and want them to finish high school. A substantial number of their children go to college.

The members of Class C do not belong much to associations outside of the churches, lodges, and labor unions.

Class D—Lower-Lower Class. This class includes the very poor, the disreputable and the demoralized. They are looked down on by the rest of the community. Even in good economic conditions some of them are unemployed, and their jobs are less stable than those of Class C.

There are a considerable number of women in this group who are raising children with little or no help from the fathers. Some of the women live on state funds through the program of Aid for Dependent Children. Others work outside of the home as waitresses, dishwashers, cleaning women, unskilled domestic workers, or unskilled workers in a local industry.

Although the adults of Class D are often semi-literate and few of them have been to high school, their children spread over a wide range of intelligence.

Although the community generally looks down upon Class D as shiftless and irresponsible, it nevertheless recognizes that some people are there through bad luck, ill health, and so forth. Some of the women who are raising children on Aid for Dependent Children would be in Class C if their husbands were living with them and supporting the family.

Democracy and the Class Structure

The story of this group of children will illustrate two opposite facts about social structure in America, which should be seen together. One fact is that the opportunities and the rewards in life are unequally distributed, more good things going to the children of higher status families. The opposite fact is that a large minority of children from lower-status families do very well in school and community, making good use of the opportunities they find, and many of them eventually rise above the social class level of their parents.

The school system, when it is well conducted, gives opportunity to lower-class children and at the same time maintains a climate of mutual trust and cooperation between children of the several social

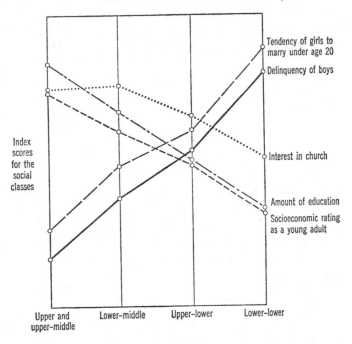

Upper and upper-middle · Lower-middle · Upper-lower · Lower-lower

Index scores for the social classes

Tendency of girls to marry under age 20
Delinquency of boys
Interest in church
Amount of education
Socioeconomic rating as a young adult

Social Class and Facts about Youth in River City

Note: The index scores have been computed from data in various tables to bring the five sets of data on to one and the same graph.

classes, which is the forerunner of harmonious working relations between the classes when the children become adults.

Although there is no class war in River City, there certainly are some hostilities between classes, and sometimes they arise in the schools, or at least they are clearly evident there. This is illustrated in the following interview with Bernice Hatfield, a girl from a lower-class family who dropped out of school before she was 16, and was married shortly afterward. The interview was made as one of a routine series on school dropouts, and is reported in the first person by the interviewer.

Bernice is living with her mother-in-law. I scaled a fifteen-foot muddy embankment up to this little run-down house. Apparently there is a more accessible route from the rear. Bernice required very little explanation. I asked her how long she had been out of school.

"I quit two weeks before the end of school a year ago. I was only fifteen at the time but I talked to Mr. McCoy (principal). He said that they wouldn't come get me because I would be sixteen before fall. I just didn't take the exams. I knew I wouldn't pass anyway because I didn't do any work except in typing. I really loved typing. It seems I didn't like all of my teachers. I got kicked out of English six times. Me and the teacher couldn't get along. I don't think half the kids liked her. She talked about the same thing for about a week and you didn't learn anything. Then she would spend the whole period with one kid. I took a dislike to her the first two days. I guess I could have gotten along with her but after that I didn't try. And then I just didn't understand general math I suppose because I don't understand arithmetic. I love it but I don't get it. I just love fractions, but those reading problems, I could never get those all the way through school. I was really going to go all the way through Home Ec because I liked it, but then my schedule was changed so I could be in a different gym class. They said they wanted to break up a gang of us girls because we were beating all the other teams and smarting off a lot. Then I got changed to a gym class with a lot of these high class girls, as we call them. They think they are better than everyone else. They got a lot of money. They don't like us and we don't like them. When my class was changed, I didn't even dress for gym. So I failed that too."

"Bernice, what seems to be the rub with those high class kids?"

"Well, they seem to look down on us kids in this neighborhood. You know, they think we are scabs. You know, those kids always hung out on the east side of the building and us kids were always on the west side. Then in class, the rich kids always had their lessons. They never came without their lessons. Then if us kids didn't have ours, and we usually didn't, they would look at us. There were only two girls, Sally Clancy and Georgia Lane that I could get along with out of that bunch. I guess it's a good thing I quit school because whenever there was any trouble, I was in the middle of it, street fights or anything else. It seems like it has been that way all my life. My temper gets me into trouble. I slap and ask questions later. That's the way my Mother and Dad were and I guess that's the way I am."

COMMUNITY AGENCIES TO ASSIST GROWTH

Every community contains a number of organizations which have as at least one important function the task of assisting boys and girls to grow up. This study attempts to record the service performed by these groups, and at the same time relies heavily upon information provided by and through these agencies.

Schools. The River City public schools were average Midwestern schools at the time of this study. Children entered the elementary school near their home at the age of five or six. Five-year-olds entered kindergarten. Six-year-olds entered first grade. They remained in the elementary school buildings until the end of the seventh grade, when they went for two years to the junior high school—one school serving the entire city. At the tenth grade they entered the senior high school. In senior high school there were courses for commercial and industrial vocations, as well as the usual college preparatory course.

There was little or no grouping of children by ability in the elementary and junior high schools. Most classes had children with a wide range of intelligence, though this range narrowed in the senior high school, and certain advanced classes in language and mathematics contained mainly students of high intelligence. Otherwise there was no grouping by ability in senior high school.

The River City schools will figure most importantly in this study because they provide the principal avenue for growing up. According to law, children must attend school until they reach the age of 16. Even after that age the chances are not good for growing up outside of the school system, though a number of boys and girls try it, as we shall see.

Churches. River City is dotted with churches of all major denominations. These churches provide religious instruction and a certain amount of social life. One of the churches conducted a Saturday night recreation program in its social hall, for teen-agers, regardless of their church affiliation. Called the "Downbeat," this program attracted quite a variety of youngsters. There are churches that have a cross-sectional slice of the social structure in their membership, and others that have a limited range of social status.

Small-Group Agencies. Especially active in River City were Boy Scouts and Girl Scouts. The unit groups of boys and girls were generally formed through a church or a school. Both organizations had active summer camp programs. There was also a YMCA program, centered around the gymnasium and swimming pool, and a YWCA club program. In addition there were some 4-H Clubs in town, a DeMolay chapter, and a Catholic Youth Organization recreation program.

Recreational Facilities. River City parks were available for unorganized picnics, tennis, and swimming. Except for the swimming pool there was no supervised recreational program. The presence of the river made boating and fishing available to boys and men of all social classes. There was also enough wild and wooded land to make hunting feasible and attractive.

A community organization in the lower-class area conducted a recreation program for youth, centering around the "Castle," a big old house on the bluff over the river which was bought and turned into a Recreation Center. Many lower-class youths preferred the dances and parties at the Castle to those given by the schools, feeling more at home and more welcome at the Castle.

Commercial recreation was of the usual type. There were motion picture theaters, roller-skating rinks, and drug stores and ice-cream parlors which were "hang-outs" for teen-agers in various parts of the city.

Library. The public library was easily accessible, and had a Children's Room for elementary school pupils.

Places of Employment. Though the shops and factories, offices, restaurants, service stations, and farms of Van Buren County have other major functions, they also provide employment and job training for youth. Some of this takes place under the auspices of the schools, but most of it is simply a part of the working of the economic system in River City. In the chapter "Work," the efficacy of this method of promoting growth is discussed.

Courts, Police, Agencies of Social Control. These agencies have their youth development significance in deterring young people from straying too far from the socially-approved avenues of growth. The chapter "Delinquency" touches on this function.

Therapeutic and Rehabilitation Services. As a means of helping youth who are in difficulty with the process of growth to adulthood, the community of River City maintains a mental health service, a guidance and counselling program in the schools, and a family service agency.

TWO BOYS

Boys and girls growing up in River City are powerfully influenced by the social structure and the social institutions that have been depicted here. To a considerable extent their future is determined by their families. But they are all different, with different personalities and patterns of ability.

For example, let us look briefly at two boys, Ray and George, both of social class B, both in the top 1 per cent in intelligence, but very different boys.

Ray. Ray is the oldest boy in a lower-middle class family, whose father and mother were good students in school, though they did not go beyond high school. His father is in the office of a manufacturing concern. The father and the mother are avid readers, and they have brought Ray into their conversation about books they have read, current affairs, and so forth.

In the sixth grade Ray was easily at the top of his class. His teacher was not surprised to find that his IQ was 143, which placed him in the top one per cent of the population. He had done consistently good work for her and for the teachers in the earlier grades. Indeed, Ray was learning so rapidly as to cause some difficulty for the teacher. He was ahead of the class in most of the subjects, and the teacher was afraid that he might become bored with school. She thought of "skipping" him into the seventh grade, but this was not accepted policy in the school system, and Ray's parents did not seem to care for the idea. In any case, the boy seemed to find plenty of things to keep him usefully occupied, and he was no bother to the teacher.

However, she felt that something should be done when Ray finished his sixth-grade arithmetic book in the middle of the year. There was no point to Ray's having to listen to her explain the lesson to the average students in the class. Yet she did not want him to go on with seventh-grade arithmetic, because she thought this might cause difficulty for Ray and his seventh-grade teacher next year.

Finally she thought of giving him an algebra book to work on. "This will keep him busy," she said. She found an algebra book, and told Ray he could work on it during arithmetic periods. But she told him that she would be busy with the arithmetic class and he must work entirely "on his own."

Several weeks later, a visitor to the class noticed Ray doing algebra while the class was doing arithmetic, and spoke to him about it.

"How are you getting along with algebra?" he asked.

"Pretty good," said Ray.

"Does your teacher help you when you have difficulty?"

"No, that was part of our bargain. She said I was to work on it without asking her to help."

"Well, what do you do when you come to some problems you don't understand?"

"Oh," said Ray, "I've found out that the best thing is to turn the page and start on a new kind of problem. Generally I can do them, and then I go back to ones that bothered me and usually I can do them, too."

Ray is now in college, and he has continued his independent

ways of learning. He is known by his classmates and by his teachers as a self-directive, ambitious boy, who only wants a chance.

George. George is also the oldest boy in a lower-middle class family. His father is a clerk in a food store. The father and mother are active church workers, and greatly respected by their neighbors. Neither had been a very good student, and neither one finished high school. They enjoy camping during their vacation, and George enjoyed this kind of activity with them.

George was in the same sixth-grade class as Ray, and had almost exactly the some IQ—144, on a group intelligence test. But George's teacher did not believe it when she learned this. "He's a bright enough boy," she said, "but he's not that bright."

George was content to get his assigned lessons, which came very easily to him. He never had to do homework, and often finished a lesson early. At such times he would pull a "comic book" out of his desk and read quietly until the next lesson was due. His teacher permitted this because "it kept him out of mischief."

George's mother once asked the school counsellor what she should do to help him. "He's so much smarter than his father and me" she said. "We just don't know how to keep him busy."

George's great interest was his newspaper business. He sold the local paper on a street corner after school. So many people went out of their way to buy papers from George that one of the school counsellors asked several of them why they did this.

"Why," they said, "It's so much pleasure to do business with him."

When he had an accident and sprained his ankle, his foot was placed in a cast, and the doctor told his mother to keep him at home when it rained, so that the cast would not get wet. George willingly stayed home from school on rainy days, but he flatly refused to take a rainy day off from his newspaper stand.

George graduated from high school in the middle of his class. He is known as an "under-achiever," because he got B's in his courses when he had the ability to make A's. He works for a local business man, who pays him well and encourages him to think of working up in the business and eventually becoming a partner.

The fact that these two boys were both brought up in lower-middle class families was important, and caused them to be alike in some ways. But they were affected differently by their particular families. They had different hereditary make-ups. They went to different churches and had different friends.

It is the resultant of all these formative influences that we are trying to trace in the lives of boys and girls in this study group.

The Problem with Which This Book Deals

This book is something more than a naturalistic description of how boys and girls grow up in a typical community. It is also an attempt to see how a community organizes its forces to give its youth a good chance to grow up into competent adults.

We know that children come into this world with differing life chances, because they have different biological potentials and because they are born into families with different social potentials.

The community provides channels of growth and aids to growth. Some questions that this book will attempt to answer are: How do the various youth-serving agencies affect the life chances of children? Do they tend to increase the life chances of those who are born with less than the average? Do they tend to serve best the ones who already have the best life chances?

2

≈≈≈

TALENT AND ABILITY

W HO ARE THE TALENTED children? What
kind of families do they come from? What are
they like, as individuals? To what extent do they develop their talent?
These are the questions we shall answer in this chapter.

Information was gathered systematically on three forms of talent:
intellectual, leadership, and artistic. These were chosen because of
their differences, and because fairly simple methods were available
to measure them.

Talent was defined as the promise of superior performance. Talent
was therefore treated as a *capacity* for *performance,* and the principal
question with which the study was concerned was: To what extent
and under what circumstances do children who show promise of
superior performance actually develop their talents? The boys and
girls who are called "talented" are the upper ten per cent of the group.

How Talent Was Measured

Intellectual talent was measured by a battery of intelligence tests
given when the boys and girls were 10 to 12 years old. Several
kinds of intelligence tests were used, to avoid a purely bookish or
academic definition of intellectual talent, and to give children with
high nonverbal intelligence a chance to qualify. In addition to the
Chicago Primary Mental Abilities Test, the following were used:

20

Thurstone Concealed Figures, Goodenough Draw-a-Man, Davis-Eells Games. Scores from the various tests were transformed into "standard scores" and then averaged in order to determine the level of intellectual talent possessed by individuals.

The measure of social leadership was the average of scores on two instruments: the Behavior Description Chart with which the teachers noted the most characteristic behavior of their pupils; and the Who Are They? sociometric test in which the children identified the leaders in their class.

For the measurement of artistic ability the Four-Drawing test was devised. Sixth grade pupils were asked in their regular classrooms to draw the following four pictures: a landscape, a classroom seen from the doorway, a free choice of something the child liked to draw, and the figure of a man. The four pictures were rated by a committee of local artists, and the boys and girls whose pictures secured the highest average ratings were named as those possessing artistic talent.

For the purpose of studying talented children, the top 10 per cent were selected in each of these three areas.

Who Are the Talented?

Girls appear about twice as often as boys on all three talent lists. This is not surprising, for it is generally known that girls do better than boys at the age of 11 in most tests of intellectual ability, and that they are regarded by their teachers and by their age-mates as more mature and better adjusted socially than boys. However, it is known that boys tend to catch up with girls in these areas during adolescence.

There is a strong tendency for boys and girls from higher-status families to appear on the talent lists more frequently than those of lower-status families. This is seen in Table 3, which shows the percentage of each social class in each talent group. However, there is no significant difference between classes A and B. This means that upper-middle and lower-middle classes produce talented children with equal frequencies. The upper-working class follows the two middle classes, whereas the lower-working class produces the lowest numbers of the talented. The class differences in Table 3 are reliable in the statistical sense.*

* Wherever differences are referred to as being real differences, they have been tested and found to be statistically significant at least at the 5 per cent level.

Thus there are talented children in all social levels, and the fact that the working class is so numerous makes it extremely important as a reservoir of talent.

Looking at the whole range of intellectual ability, one sees that intelligence as measured by the tests is distributed quite unequally among the social classes. Table 3A shows the relation between social class and intelligence at the sixth-grade level. The middle social classes have far more than half of their members above average in

TABLE 3A. SOCIAL CLASS AND TALENT

		Boys				Girls		
Class	Number	% in Talent Group			Number	% in Talent Group		
		Intelligence	Leadership	Arts		Intelligence	Leadership	Art
A	21	15	15	5	22	34	32	14
B	63	11	11	5	62	34	31	26
C	91	4	7	10	94	6	8	7
D	68	6	0	3	58	0	5	3
Total	242	7	6	6	236	14	15	12

TABLE 3B. SOCIAL CLASS AND INTELLIGENCE

Intelligence Quartile	Per cent of each social class in each Quartile			
	Male			
	A	B	C	D
IV (High)	33%	26%	16%	11%
III	48	27	28	16
II	19	31	26	32
I	0	16	30	41
Number	22	62	91	62
	Female			
	A	B	C	D
IV	62%	44%	19%	7%
III	14	25	28	20
II	5	20	30	40
I	19	11	23	33
Number	21	64	94	58

intelligence, whereas the lower classes have more than half of their members below average. This relation is expressed by correlation coefficients of .34 and .28 between socio-economic status and intelligence for sixth grade boys and girls respectively.

Overlapping of Talents

There is a considerable degree of overlapping of talents. That is, a person may appear on two or even three talent lists. Twelve girls and four boys appear on all three lists, whereas by mathematical probability there would be only one person on all three lists among a group of 1,000 people, which is the size of the group being studied. Table 4 shows the amount of overlapping among the talent groups

TABLE 4. OVERLAPPING OF THE TALENT GROUPS (1,015 CHILDREN)

Characteristic	Leadership	Intelligence
	(N = 104)	(N = 107)
Intelligence (N = 107)		
No. of overlaps observed	45	
No. expected on basis of chance	11	
Artistic Talent (N = 102)		
No. of overlaps observed	31	33
No. expected on basis of chance	11	11

Note: The numbers expected by chance are calculated with the assumption that there is no systematic correlation of talents.

when they are taken in pairs. This table actually refers to two River City groups totalling 1,000 children. One group is the particular subject of this book, and the other group was two years younger. There was about the same degree of overlapping of talent in the two groups, and consequently they were combined in this table. In general, there is three to four times as much overlapping of talent as would occur if there was no systematic correlation among the three types of talent.* If there had been no overlapping of talent, there would have been 313 children out of 1,015 or about 30 per

* Another measure of overlapping of talent is given by the coefficient of correlation of the measures of intelligence and leadership, which is .37 for boys and .49 for girls in the group being studied.

cent identified as talented by this method. However, the number actually identified was 220 or 22 per cent of the total group.

Intelligence, Sex, and Age

It has already been noted that girls outnumber boys among the top 10 per cent on intelligence tests in the sixth grade. The same group was tested again in the junior year of high school, five years later, with a group test of intellectual development that was part of the state-wide testing program. This was the Differential Aptitude Test. Although this test was not identical with those used earlier, it is interesting to study the relation of scores on the earlier sixth-grade test battery to scores on the eleventh-grade test. The correlation co-efficients between the two scores are .74 for girls and .70 for boys, for the 254 boys and girls who took both sets of tests.

More than half of the top 10 per cent at the sixth grade were still in the top 10 per cent on the eleventh grade test, and the remainder were practically all in the upper quarter. About a third of those in the upper tenth at the eleventh grade were below the upper tenth at the sixth grade, but practically all were in the upper quarter of the sixth grade.

Table 5 shows the distribution of boys and girls among the top scorers at the two age levels, and tells something about the relations between age, sex, and intellectual talent. The scores in Table 5 are T-scores, with a score of 65 falling at the 93 percentile, and 55 falling

TABLE 5. COMPARISON OF BOYS AND GIRLS IN INTELLECTUAL APTITUDE AT GRADES 6 AND 11

T-score for Intellectual Aptitude	Grade 6		Grade 11	
	Boys	Girls	Boys	Girls
70+	4	4	5	4
65–69	10	12	5	9
60–64	10	22	13	17
55–59	32	33	18	20
Total	56	71	41	50

Note: T-scores for grade 6 were based on this study group only; T-scores for grade 11 were based on state-wide norms.

at the 70 percentile.   The girls outnumber the boys principally in the
range between 60 and 69 at both grade levels.   There is no statistically
reliable difference between the ratios of the sexes at the two ages,
though the boys show a slight tendency to catch up with the girls as
they grow older.

Community Conditions for the Development of Talent

The question whether a boy or girl develops his or her talent is
decided by a number of factors, some within the youth, and some outside of him.   These are discussed in some detail in a later chapter, but
here it is interesting to consider certain community factors as they influence the development of talent in the arts.

River City is known as a music-loving community.   There is a good
local symphony orchestra, and the community is enthusiastic about the
music program in elementary and secondary schools, aimed at develop-
ing instrumental and vocal musical abilities.   There are public per-
formances by school orchestra, band, and chorus, and regional and
state musical contests are fully reported in the newspaper with pictures of the boys and girls who participate.   These factors tend to
stimulate boys and girls with musical aptitude to develop their talents.

Some idea of the extent to which community conditions favor the
development of musical talent is given by the following accounts of
the development of musical talent in a boy and a girl.

Earl.   Earl Lawson is the son of a working-class family with many
children, all of whom have done well in school, although only one
of his older brothers has gone to college.   Earl has good intellectual
ability but has always paid more attention to his music than to his
other studies.   Although there was no tradition of musical talent in
the family, Earl showed an interest as early as the fifth grade and
did so well in the school orchestra that his teacher visited his home
and urged his parents to get him a horn of his own.   They found a
cheap second-hand cornet for Earl, who went on to master several
other instruments and to play the piano.   In high school he took a
leading part in the orchestra and was very close to the director,
who encouraged him to plan to go to college and to prepare for becoming a teacher of music.   Earl now is doing good work in college,
earning enough to supplement a small scholarship since his parents
cannot afford to help him financially.

Lorraine.   Lorraine French started music as soon as she started school
and was playing the piano rather well by the time she was in the

fourth grade. Her father, a college graduate employed in the office of a local factory, enjoys music, has decided preferences for what he calls "good" music, and has kept Lorraine at her practicing whenever she showed signs of becoming impatient. He has personally sought out the best teachers he could find for her in the community.

Lorraine enjoyed school work and did uniformly well in all school subjects. She had a preference for art, and took lessons in a Saturday morning painting and drawing class when she was in junior high school. But music remained her main interest, and by the time she was in the sixth grade she was doing well on the violin as well as piano; shortly afterward she commenced to play the organ at her church.

In junior high school she joined the high school orchestra, and commenced a series of appearances in the state high school music contests where she received superior ratings throughout the rest of her school career. During the summers she attended special music sessions at colleges in the region. Perhaps her culminating achievement was to appear as a soloist with the River City Symphony while she was still in high school.

In addition to her father's interest in her musical career, Lorraine found that she was appreciated in school and in her church for this talent, and she was frequently mentioned in the local newspaper for her accomplishments.

Children with talent in the other arts get less community backing and reward. The community is not so appreciative of talent in painting and in dramatics, for example. The schools do not systematically promote work in other arts, as they do in music.

Yet there has been some recent effort to promote the development of children's talent in these other fields. A Children's Theater has come into existence with an active summer program. This has come too late to serve the children of the study group, but it has stimulated some of the younger children. Also, a Society for Fine Arts has recently been established, aimed to promote appreciation of and creative work in a variety of arts. As these community organizations develop, their influence will be felt in the schools, and they will create an atmosphere more favorable to the development of incipient talent in all the arts.

Perhaps the story of a boy like Donald Davenport will have a happier ending as these community forces gain strength.

Donald.   Donald is a member of the study group, raised in a working-class family.   He has above average general intelligence and very good drawing ability.   On the screening tests for art ability in the sixth grade, he was a stand-out.   He is definitely a talented boy, with test scores indicating that he can do very well in occupations involving drawing ability and spatial imagery—such occupations as mechanical engineer, architect, artist, or draftsman.

In elementary school there was no art teacher and Donald's talent was not developed.   In junior high school he enjoyed his work in art and industrial art, and always served on committees for decorating the gymnasium when they had school parties.   Neither the industrial arts nor the fine arts teacher seems to have paid particular attention to Donald, who told an interviewer that as an industrial arts project he had worked hard on a small rocking chair.   "I made that little rocker over there.   I got a little mad over the deal.   I designed my pattern and made it out of hard wood.   It was slow going.   While I did that, the other guys made a lot of those little wall gadgets, following the teacher's pattern.   They got better grades than I did because they made so many of them."

Donald lost interest in school, and shortly after he was 16 he bought an automobile which required such heavy payments that he found it easy to quit school and work full time.   Three years later, at 19, Donald had made no progress toward a career.   He had held several jobs at unskilled work, and was currently working as a delivery man for a furniture store.   On two or three occasions he had been allowed to help in arranging the show window, and his employer remarked that Donald had good taste in furniture design.

If Donald's talent had been in music, it is likely that he would have been encouraged and assisted to develop his ability, and perhaps to become a musician.

Generally speaking, a community like River City concentrates on helping boys and girls develop their intellectual abilities, with a good deal of supplementary emphasis on musical talent.   Athletic talent is also sought out and cultivated in River City.   But River City does not do as much to encourage the development of other nonintellectual talent, such as painting, the dance, creative writing, dramatics.

These special talents are likely to be cultivated only when a family is interested in them and encourages a child, or, more rarely, when a school teacher discovers a talented youth and encourages both him and his family.

3

≈≈≈

PERSONAL AND SOCIAL
ADJUSTMENT

THE PURPOSE OF THIS CHAPTER is to look at
good and poor social and emotional adjustment of
the boys and girls in the study group while they were in school and
to show how adjustment is related to other characteristics of these
children. This chapter tells how adjustment was measured and
focuses on the nature of social and emotional life in childhood and
adolescence in River City. Other chapters tell how social and emotional or personal adjustment is related to success and failure in growing up.

What Is Adjustment?

The child who gets a good start in life has an active, inquiring mind
and also a mind that is at peace with itself. This double-sided statement is the basic proposition of this book. We shall see that the
children who became the most competent adolescents and young
adults were those with these two qualities of mind.

By a "mind at peace with itself" we do not mean a sleepy mind, or
one that has no uncertainties within itself and no conflicts with the
world it faces. We mean a mind that is wide awake, sensitive, and

sometimes discontented with things; nevertheless a mind that has an inner harmony of forces making up the personality.

The person who has this kind of mind has good personal or emotional adjustment. In a reasonably good society this person also has good social adjustment. In order to study personal and social adjustment it was necessary to study the children's group—the peer group. The child's position in the peer group was thought to have the same order of importance as his standing on an intelligence test.

Good adjustment was defined for the purposes of the study as pleasant relations with other boys and girls and with teachers, in which the child was able to "be himself," to have friends, to be a leader as well as a follower, and to be confident of his own worth. One aspect of good adjustment was called *Social Leadership*, though it was probably not so much leadership as social effectiveness. The scores for social leadership had a correlation coefficient of .75 with scores for *Friendship*, which were simply the numbers of boys and girls who listed the individual as one they would like for a friend, on a sociometric test. Other instruments for the measurement of adjustment carried their own operational definitions of good adjustment which are discussed when they are brought into this chapter.

Poor adjustment is seen by psychologists to take two general forms, one being aggressive and the other passive or withdrawn behavior. These general forms can be divided into other more specific forms of maladjustment, but this did not seem useful in this particular study. Aggressive maladjustment consists of behavior in which a person is hostile to others, breaks rules, destroys property, steals, fights and quarrels. Withdrawn maladjustment consists of behavior in which a person is shy, fearful, and seclusive.

Good and poor personal-social adjustment were measured by two procedures. One, using a sociometric test called the Who Are They? test (WAT) asks all the children in a classroom or a homeroom to name the children who best fit certain thumbnail descriptions. For leadership, such items as the following were used: "Who are the leaders, the leaders in several things?"; "Who are the ones that have good ideas of interesting things to do?" For the friendship score, the children answered the question, "Who would you like for your best friends?" The number of times a given child was mentioned was his score.

For aggressive maladjustment, the WAT contained several items such as: "Which boys and girls quarrel and get mad easily?" and "Who are the boys and girls that break rules—rules of the school and rules of games?" The following questions are typical of those that contributed to the withdrawn maladjustment score: "Who are the ones that are too shy to make friends easily?" and "Who are the boys and girls that stay out of games? They don't like to play hard."

The other procedure called on the teacher's observation of her pupils, without asking her to make a moral judgment concerning them. The Behavior Description Chart is a "forced-choice" type instrument which asks the teacher to pick the items "most like" and "least like" a given child in a set of ten groups of five statements each such as the following:

A. Other people find it hard to get along with him
B. Is very shy
C. Other people are eager to be near him or on his side
D. Is usually willing to go along with the group
E. Interested in other people's opinions and activities

In the foregoing pentad, if A was marked as "most like" a given child, it contributed to his score for aggressiveness. If B was "most like" him, it contributed to his score for withdrawal. Item C was a leadership item, and D and E were not scored because they are often applied by teachers to average children with respect to social adjustment. Similarly, a "least like" nomination for A, B, or C subtracted from the child's score on that variable.

The sociometric test was administered in sixth and seventh-grade classrooms and the ninth-grade homeroom (since the ninth-grade work was departmentalized). The Behavior Description Chart was filled out by the teachers of these classes at the same times. The scores on these instruments were turned into percentiles, and the two percentiles for each adjustment variable were averaged to arrive at the leadership and maladjustment scores.

In the sixth and seventh grades the children attended schools that were relatively homogeneous with respect to socioeconomic status. It was thought that from the various schools this would lead to the identification of approximately the same percentages of children as leaders, aggressive, or withdrawn, as children and teachers would be judging a given child against others in the classroom rather than against the entire citywide population of children. However, the average leadership scores on both the Behavior Description Chart and the Who Are They? were higher in the middle-class schools than in the working-class schools; whereas the average scores for aggressive and withdrawn maladjustment were lower in middle-class schools than in working-class schools.

Three other measures of psychological adjustment were used in the study. The *California Test of Personality* was given each child in the seventh grade. This is a self-report inventory. Its validity is open to considerable question, especially after the eighth grade, and middle-class children do better on it than do lower-class children because of the systematic bias in some of the items. Data from this test are not reported here, but they give statistical support to the other measures of psychological adjustment.

In the tenth grade the *California Psychological Inventory (CPI)* was administered to all boys and girls still in school at that time. This is a self-report instrument that avoids some of the disadvantages of the California Test of Personality by using items not so obviously aimed at the adjustment area. The CPI is designed to measure such characteristics as responsibility, intellectual efficiency, self-assurance, and ascendance. It also gives a single total score which can be used as a measure of personal-social adjustment.

Also in the tenth grade a projective *Sentence Completion Test* (SCT) was given, to measure maturity of approach to four developmental tasks that adolescents are seeking to master: learning a masculine or feminine social-sex role, becoming autonomous or self-directing, accepting oneself as a worthwhile person, and accepting and respecting other people.

The Configurations of Good and Poor Adjustment

The relationships among these measures of adjustment and between them and socioeconomic status and intelligence are shown in Table 6, which presents product-moment correlations for each sex taken separately. This table shows that aggressiveness and withdrawal are negatively correlated with each other, being different types of maladjustment. They are also negatively correlated with all the measures of good adjustment and with socio-economic status and intelligence.

The only exception to this rule is that aggressiveness in girls is not reliably related to any of the good-adjustment scores, either positively or negatively. This is probably because few girls get high aggressiveness scores, and a moderate aggression score in a girl signifies a dominating and outgoing personality with or without much hostility. Thus aggressiveness in girls as measured by these instruments is not an indication of maladjustment, except for a few girls with very high aggression scores.

Withdrawal scores for both boys and girls have generally higher negative correlation coefficients with measures of good personal adjustment than aggression scores do.   However, as is shown in the chapter, "Delinquency," aggression scores are highly related to delinquency in boys.   The withdrawal score is probably a better index of *personal*

TABLE 6. THE CONFIGURATION OF GOOD AND POOR ADJUSTMENT (PRODUCT-MOMENT CORRELATION COEFFICIENTS)

Girls (N = 150)

		ISC	IQ	L	F	Agg	Wi	CPI	Self	Auto	Others	Sex Role
	ISC	X	34	41	43	11	−37	43	27	16	13	17
	IQ	28	X	49	25	05	−45	54	31	24	13	10
	L	25	37	X	76	−05	−76	54	46	36	37	25
Boys	F	21	18	70	X	10	−58	36	31	18	29	41
N = 137	Agg	−10	−11	−23	−13	X	−22	08	−09	−01	−10	−08
	Wi	−08	−28	−61	−45	−24	X	−51	−37	−36	−23	−22
	CPI	22	32	48	40	−19	−22	X	46	47	42	32
SCT {	Self	16	15	31	31	−15	−05	55	X	61	57	44
	Auto	18	35	39	31	−16	−21	56	62	X	39	16
	Others	18	14	33	28	−28	−20	56	48	49	X	57
	Sex Role	23	22	32	36	−07	−28	43	34	37	55	X

Notes: Decimal points have been omitted. Coefficients greater than .21 are significant at the .01 level; greater than .16 are significant at the .05 level.
ISC = Socioeconomic status of parents
IQ = intelligence measures in sixth and seventh grades
L, F, Agg, Wi are leadership, friendship, aggression, and withdrawal, measured in the ninth grade.
CPI = California Psychological Inventory in tenth grade
SCT variables in the tenth grade; Acceptance of *Self*, *Autonomy*, Acceptance of *Others*, Acceptance of *Sex role*.

maladjustment than is the aggression score for boys and girls, whereas the aggression score is a better predictor of a particular form of *social* maladjustment (delinquency) among boys.

As is seen in subsequent chapters, social and personal maladjustment is closely related to dropping out of school, and to underachievement in school.   Later chapters also show that maladjustment in childhood and early adolescence is closely related to maladjustment at work, in marriage, in college, and to delinquency.

Talent and Maladjustment

There is very little overlapping of talent and maladjustment. None of the 50 most aggressive children or the 48 most withdrawn children was seen as having sufficient social leadership to be in the 50 who were highest on that score. Of the 50 most aggressive, only one boy was among the 50 with highest IQ; of the 48 most withdrawn children, 3 girls were also in the 50 with highest IQ.

On the other hand, as was seen in the chapter on talent, there was a great deal of overlapping of high social leadership scores, or good adjustment, with intellectual and artistic talent.

Characteristics of Those with Especially Good or Poor Adjustment

On the basis of the teacher ratings and sociometric tests (BDC and WAT) the 10 per cent who were highest in social leadership were selected for special study, and the same thing was done for the 10 per cent who were highest in aggression and in withdrawal. Thus there were three groups of approximately 50 apiece, and constituting about 30 per cent of the total group. There was no overlapping between the social leadership group and the two maladjustment groups, but these two latter groups had a small number of mutual members so that there were 92 different children in the two groups.

Table 7 shows the social class membership of those with especially good or poor adjustment. From this table it is evident that the lowest social class has a concentration of maladjustment out of proportion to its size; the highest two social groups have a similar concentration of social leadership. Table 7 also shows the difference between the

TABLE 7. SOCIAL CLASS OF SIXTH AND SEVENTH GRADE CHILDREN IN TOP TEN PER CENT IN SOCIAL LEADERSHIP, AGGRESSIVE AND WITHDRAWN MALADJUSTMENT

Social Class	Aggression		Withdrawal		Social Leadership	
	Male	Female	Male	Female	Male	Female
A	0	1	1	2	2	7
B	7	4	2	5	7	21
C	12	3	8	12	7	7
D	15	8	8	11	0	3
Total No.	34	16	19	30	16	39

sexes in the behavioral form which maladjustment takes. Boys were much more likely to show aggressive maladjustment, and girls were more likely to show withdrawn maladjustment. Girls were more likely than boys to get high social-leadership scores at the sixth and seventh grades.

Both of the maladjustment groups contained many lower-class children with below average intelligence, as can be seen in Table 8. Only one aggressive child and three withdrawn children were upper-middle class, and only one aggressive child and six withdrawn children were in the top quarter in intelligence. On the other hand, the high

TABLE 8. AGGRESSIVE AND WITHDRAWN AND HIGH-LEADERSHIP CHILDREN IN RELATION TO INTELLIGENCE AND SOCIAL CLASS

| | Top 10 per cent in: | | | | | |
	Aggression		Withdrawal		Leadership	
	Above Average IQ	Below Average IQ	Above Average IQ	Below Average IQ	Above Average IQ	Below Average IQ
Middle class	3	8	8	4	34	3
Lower class	8	23	6	27	15	2

social leadership group was predominantly above average in IQ, and heavily middle class in composition.

As there were two instruments that permitted a child to report on his own personal adjustment, it is possible to compare self-reports with judgments of peers and teachers. This shows that those who were identified by their peers and teachers as being aggressive or withdrawn also tend to see themselves as maladjusted. This was true in the seventh grade when the California Test of Personality was given. Almost half of those who were rated in the top 10 per cent on aggressive or withdrawn maladjustment rated themselves in the bottom quarter of the group on personal adjustment. On the other hand, only 3 of the 50 most aggressive children and none of the 48 most withdrawn children rated themselves in the top quarter of the group on personal adjustment. Table 9 shows that those in the top 10 per cent in social leadership tended strongly to be in the top quarter on the California Test of Personality and the California Psychological Inventory.

Children identified as maladjusted came typically from unstable families. Both maladjusted groups had twice as high a proportion of homes broken by divorce or separation as was true of the rest of the population.

Those with especially good personal-social adjustment are rather similar as a group to those with intellectual talent, as can be seen in Table 9, where the 55 with highest social leadership and the 33 with highest IQ's are compared for social class and personal adjustment as

TABLE 9. RELATIONS OF HIGH SCORES IN SOCIAL LEAD-ERSHIP AND INTELLECTUAL TALENT WITH SOCIAL CLASS AND PERSONAL ADJUSTMENT (PERCENTAGES OF THE RESPECTIVE GROUPS ARE SHOWN.)

| | | | Social Class of Parents | | | | Adjustment Score on: | | | | | | | |
| | | | | | | | California Test of Personality | | | | California Psychological Inventory | | | |
	No.	Boys	A	B	C	D	Q_4 high	Q_3	Q_2	Q_1	Q_4 high	Q_3	Q_2	Q_1
Total group	487	51	9	26	38	26	25	25	25	25	25	25	25	25
Leadership	55	33	18	51	26	5	65	24	9	2	61	27	12	0
Intellect	33	27	27	49	15	9	64	20	12	4	48	40	12	0

measured in the seventh grade by the California Personality Test and in the tenth grade by the California Psychological Inventory.

Conclusions

Personal and social adjustment takes its place beside socioeconomic status and intellectual ability as probably predictive of success or failure in school and in the tasks of growing up in River City. It is not clear which elements are more deeply causal, but it seems clear that the foregoing three factors interact to make for success or failure. The best equipment for satisfactory growth is to have a keen mind, to accept oneself and be well accepted by others, and to come from a middle-class family. But some children will probably succeed with two of these three favorable characteristics.

4
≈≈≈

ACHIEVEMENT IN SCHOOL

THE SCHOOL is a place where children grow. It is both a stage on which the drama of growth unfolds, and a set of intellectual and social forces that stimulate and guide growth. Thus it can be considered neutrally as a place where the forces of family background, intelligence, and personal adjustment combine to produce growth; and it can be considered positively as a set of stimuli coming from teachers, age-mates, books, and laboratories which force and direct the growth of the child. Both ways of looking at the school are used in this chapter.

Achievement in school is measured in River City, as in all American cities, by a system of promotion based on marks or grades given by teachers. A pupil succeeds by meeting the expectations of the teacher who observes his progress constantly and tests his knowledge periodically. He is expected to attend school regularly, to do his assigned work promptly, to behave properly. If he does these things, he gets a grade of "average." If his work is unusually good in quality or quantity, he gets a grade of "superior." If he does not accomplish much of the assigned work, or if the quality of his work is unsatisfactory, he gets a grade of "poor." About 20 per cent of the school children in River City fail one or more grades by the time they reach high school. Then, with marks given in specific subjects, failures become more frequent during the ninth and tenth grades, when about a fifth of the children drop out of school.

Because the promotion policy is liberal, there is a wide range of performance and knowledge within a particular grade, and within a particular classroom, for River City did not group elementary and junior-high children by ability during the 1950's. Thus in a particular seventh-grade classroom, there may be some pupils reading at a fourth-grade level and others at tenth-grade level.

Furthermore, there are different levels of achievement among the different schools. Schools from the "Country Club" district have a much higher level of academic achievement than do schools from the working-class district. This was seen quite clearly when a comparison was made of two classrooms of children who graduated from their respective elementary schools and entered the eighth grade of the junior high school together.

A Comparison of Children from Contrasting Elementary Schools in the Same Junior High School

The less-privileged school will be called school L, and the school from a predominantly upper-middle class district will be called school M. During the eighth and ninth grades, the children from school L were absent 4.5 times as often as those from school M, and tardy 4.9 times as often. As for failures in school subjects, not one child from school M failed in any subject during the eighth and ninth grades; the pupils from school L failed an average of one subject in the eighth grade and one and a half subjects in the ninth grade.

Among the "academic" subjects of English, Mathematics, Civics, Science, and Journalism taken in the ninth grade, 45 per cent of the grades made by children from school M were A's, whereas not a single A was earned by a child from school L. Among the less "academic" subjects of home economics, industrial arts, speech, dramatics, typewriting, agriculture, art, and music, 62 per cent of the grades made by children from school M were A's, while 7 per cent of the grades of children from school L were A's. Even in physical education there was a difference of the same type between the marks of children from the two different schools.

At the time of graduation from high school, no one from school L had better than a C+ average in academic subjects, and most of the group had dropped out of school. On the other hand, over a third of the children from school M had an A or A— average, and only two children had averages below C—.

In the same way there was a difference in social adjustment of pupils from the two schools. When the total group of ninth grade pupils in the junior high school rated their peers on the Who Are They? test, they gave an average of 70 nominations per child from school M on social leadership items, and an average of 5 nominations per child from school L.

Thus the academic and social performance of the children from the upper-middle class school is far superior to that of the children from the lower class school.

Characteristics Related to Achievement in High School

Looking at all the sixth graders, rather than only those from these two contrasting schools, we can see in Tables 10, 11, and 12 that the promise of good or poor' achievement in high school was clearly present in the elementary school. Scholastic achievement in high school is measured in terms of rank at the end of the eleventh grade, based on an average of the student's school marks in the ninth, tenth, and eleventh grades.

Table 10 shows the correlation coefficients between high-school rank and sixth-grade school marks, social adjustment, intelligence quotient, and socioeconomic status. The coefficients for intelligence and for

TABLE 10. CORRELATIONS BETWEEN CHARACTERISTICS OF 6TH GRADERS AND THEIR HIGH-SCHOOL MARKS. (SIXTH-GRADE DATA.)

Rank in High School	Socio-economic Status	IQ	School Marks	Social Leader-ship	Aggres-siveness	With-drawal
Boys ($N = 145$)	.40	.59	.76	.46	$-.30$	$-.26$
Girls ($N = 154$)	.45	.59	.72	.57	$-.32$	$-.40$

Note: This table refers only to boys and girls who were in school in the sixth grade and were still there in the eleventh grade. The IQ is based on the Chicago Primary Abilities Test. The correlation coefficient for school marks in the sixth grade is a bi-serial coefficient, and possibly overestimates the true relationship. The other correlation coefficients are computed by the product-moment formula. The numbers of boys and girls with scores on Leadership, Aggressiveness and Withdrawal were 100 boys and 111 girls. The coefficient of correlation between personal adjustment as measured by the California Psychological Inventory in the ninth grade and high-school marks was .60 for boys and .56 for girls.

school marks are somewhat higher than those for social status and social adjustment. Thus high-school academic achievement can be said to be closely related to a composite of family background (social class), intelligence, and personal-social adjustment.

The relation between IQ in the sixth grade, and high-school rank is shown in more detail in Table 11. The tendency is strong for those

TABLE 11. RELATION BETWEEN IQ IN SIXTH GRADE AND SCHOOL MARKS IN HIGH SCHOOL

	No. in Each Quartile of IQ in Sixth Grade				
School Marks in 11th grade	IV (high)	III	II	I	Total
Top 50 pupils					
Boys	14	1	0	0	15
Girls	24	9	1	1	35
Next 50 pupils					
Boys	10	6	1	1	18
Girls	17	7	6	2	32

Quartile in High-School Marks	Percentages from each Quartile of IQ in Sixth Grade			
IV (high)	58	14	3	3
III	29	36	24	8
II	6	30	41	38
I	7	20	32	51
Total	100	100	100	100

Note: There were 362 pupils in the eleventh grade. This table refers to the sixth graders who were still in school in the eleventh grade. Therefore it omits those who dropped out of school before the eleventh grade.

in a given quartile of IQ in the sixth grade to be in the same quartile of high school rank in the eleventh grade.

The relation between social adjustment as measured by the social-leadership score in the ninth grade and high-school rank is shown in Table 12. This relation is of the same order of magnitude as the relation between IQ and high-school rank. The 92 children who were in the 10 per cent most aggressive or most withdrawn have been especially unsuccessful in school. As compared with the total group, twice as many aggressive children have failed to pass at least one grade during their school careers; three times as many withdrawn children have failed in school. Only a third of the withdrawn

TABLE 12. RELATION BETWEEN SOCIAL ADJUSTMENT AND HIGH-SCHOOL MARKS

High-School Rank in School Marks by Quartiles

Quartile for Social Leadership	IV (high)	III	II	I	No Information	Total No.
Boys						
IV (high)	13	16	6	3	10	48
III	5	10	16	9	16	56
II	3	1	13	13	37	67
I	0	3	3	15	46	67
No information	0	0	1	0	8	9
Total no.	21	30	39	40	117	247
Girls						
IV	30	16	2	1	21	70
III	12	12	11	10	17	62
II	4	4	10	10	23	51
I	1	1	5	10	34	51
No information	0	0	1	0	5	6
Total no.	47	33	29	31	100	240
Total Group						
IV	43	32	8	4	31	118
III	17	22	27	19	33	118
II	7	5	23	23	60	118
I	1	4	8	25	80	118
No information	0	0	2	0	13	15
Total no.	68	63	68	71	217	487

Note: The "no information" column is large because only those who were still in school in the eleventh grade comprise the group for whom rank in class was calculated. The social leadership data were obtained in the ninth grade.

children were still in school at the end of the eleventh grade, and of those remaining more than half were in the bottom quarter of the class. The aggressive children left school even earlier. Two-fifths had left by the end of the ninth grade and only 1 in 5 graduated

from high school.   Only 3 children out of the 92 in the maladjustment groups went to college.

Forms of School Failure

There are three familiar types of failing pupil in River City.   The
first category is made up largely of boys who show aggressive social
maladjustment as well as poor learning ability.   This type is described
with illustrations in the chapter on delinquency, for these youngsters,
if they are boys, have a high probability of becoming delinquent.

The second type has a majority of girls and shows withdrawn
maladjustment as well as poor learning ability.   An example of
a girl of this type is Myrna.   In the sixth grade she was identified
by the Who Are They? test as a withdrawn child—one who was shy,
afraid to speak in class, and seen by her classmates as afraid to
play games.   Yet she was two years older than the rest of the class,
having failed twice in school because she could not read.   She was
getting some individual tutoring by a remedial reading teacher
but making poor progress.   She was absent from school a great deal
of the time due to stomach upsets, though the doctor could not find
anything physically wrong with her.

Myrna.   Myrna was a pretty, blonde, blue-eyed girl, attractive to her
teachers who felt baffled in their attempts to help her.   At home
there was her mother, a step-father, and a small sister who was
a child of her mother's present marriage.   The mother complained
about Myrna's poor health and encouraged her to stay home when
she felt ill.   The mother also complained about her husband,
who she said was neglecting her.   The step-father was a factory
worker, a fairly steady man but quite harsh in his treatment of
Myrna and sometimes cruel to his wife.

Eventually Myrna reached the ninth grade at the age of 16.   By
this time she was grown-up physically but quite incapable of doing
high-school work.   She was reading at about the fourth-grade
level and was discouraged about herself.   She was convinced she
was stupid, and she was so unsure of herself that she avoided talking
to adults in the school for fear that they would make too great de-
mands on her.   For example, when a sweater was stolen from her
locker, she did not report it to the office because she thought the
secretary would ask her questions she could not answer.   She said to
her counselor, "Oh, I'm so dumb, I don't like to talk to people be-

cause they'll find out how dumb I am." In her home economics class she was sewing on a piece of clothing and had some difficulty with it. Rather than ask the teacher for help, she sat and did nothing for several days, and finally took an "F" for the grading period.

At home things were going poorly for Myrna. Boys were asking her for dates, but her mother was suspicious of them all and made it unpleasant for them if they came to the house. One boy, a senior in high school, persisted in going with Myrna, and her mother made it extremely difficult for them to be alone together. If the boy came to the home, her mother would watch them like a hawk and accuse Myrna of all kinds of bad conduct if they so much as went out into the hall to be alone. If they went out to a movie, her mother would set a time for her to get home and would be waiting for them, to send the boy away as soon as they arrived home.

Once when Myrna tried to argue with her mother, the mother told her that she was illegitimate, that she tried to get rid of Myrna before she was born, and that now she wanted to protect Myrna from having the same thing happen to her. Speaking to her counselor after this, Myrna said that she was all mixed up, and tired of life. She did not see anything to this living business anyway; you were born and grew up, and then you got married and had children and got tired and disgusted with life.

A third type of unsuccessful pupil does not fail in school but simply displays lack of interest. For example, there was a lower-class boy of high ability and good social adjustment who had done well throughout elementary school, but decided to drop out of school during the tenth grade. When his counselor talked with him, trying to interest him in completing high school, the boy replied, "My brother left school three years ago, and now he is a brick layer. He works six to eight hours a day and makes more money than you do. He doesn't have to grade papers at night. He has a job the year round and doesn't have to go to school in the summer. I have a chance to be an apprentice brick layer. What more could I want?"

Motivation for Educational Achievement

The third type of failure to do well in school illustrates the importance of *motivation*. The boy just mentioned had good intelligence and good social adjustment in school, but still he did not care to go on with his education. His lack of motivation may be laid to his lower-class family background, but there are some with a middle-class background, better than average in intelligence and better than average in adjustment, who also lack motivation to do well in school. On the other hand, there are a few with lower-class background, below-average intelligence, and below-average adjustment who succeed fairly well in school and go on to graduate from high school at least.

Therefore, motivation for education is something more than a composite of social class, intelligence, and personal-social adjustment, although it is closely correlated with these factors.

Motivation, or personal incentive, for education arises from the following factors which were studied in this research.

1. Need or drive for achievement.
2. Identification with a person or persons who have gone to college or have done well in school.
3. Social pressure on the individual.
4. Intrinsic pleasure in learning.

Need for Achievement. There seems to exist in some people a basic unconscious need for achievement that drives them to achieve as well as they possibly can in almost everything they undertake. McClelland* and his colleagues have defined this concept, and measured need for achievement by means of a "thematic apperception test." In this test students looked at pictures showing young men in situations where they might be undertaking some task, and then wrote brief stories on what they thought the young men were doing. For instance, a picture might show a young man in a white coat standing before a desk and holding a small object up in front of him. This might be seen as a young chemist analyzing a substance, or a young man studying to be a doctor, or any of a number of other things. The story is scored on the basis of the kind of ideas and the number of them that deal with achievement of a goal, of striving to succeed, and getting ahead in the world. This need for achievement is a deep and possibly unconscious drive of which a person may not be fully aware. Therefore it is necessary to measure it by some indirect method, such as the McClelland test.

Identification with Persons Who Have Gone to College or Done Well in School. It is likely that a boy or girl will do his best in school

* David C. McClelland, et al., *The Achievement Motive.* New York: Appleton-Century-Crofts, 1953. Bernard C. Rosen and Roy O'Andrade, "The Psychosocial Origins of Achievement Motivation." *Sociometry* 22:185–218 (1959).

if he is closely identified with another person, usually a parent, who has done well in school. The process of psychological identification of a child with an older person who is loved and trusted is well known. The child imitates the person or persons whom he identifies, and therefore attempts to do well in school if he sees this as important in the life of that person or those persons. To get information on identifications, the student was asked which adults had been most influential in his life, and then he was asked about their educational experience and whether they had urged him to go to college.

Social Pressure. There is also a number of pressures upon an individual of which he is conscious and which can easily be seen, in addition to the unconscious pressure of identification. The family, friends, teachers, and community have expectations concerning school achievement, high school graduation, and going to college, and these expectations act as pressures upon the individual. Such pressure was studied by asking the student how far his parents and his friends wished him to go in school, and what other pressures he felt that pushed him toward or away from school achievement.

Intrinsic Pleasure in Learning. It seems obvious that a person who enjoys studying and learning will do as well as his ability permits him to do in school. Probably this element of motivation is more important in the development of artistic and musical ability in River City children than in their school achievement at the elementary and secondary school levels. Probably it will have more to do with their going to college and with their achievement in college. Intrinsic pleasure in learning may play a large part in achievement in areas and at ages where the social pressure element is lacking.

Correlates of Achievement in Able High-School Youth

With the foregoing theory of what enters into school achievement a study was made of the boys and girls who were in the top third of the group in intelligence. These were divided into two groups, each with approximately the same level of intellectual ability. One group consisted of the half who made the better school marks; the other group made relatively poorer school marks. These two groups were called the *Achievers* and *Nonachievers*, respectively, and they were studied while they were in the twelfth grade. By comparing these two groups it is possible to find out what factors are associated with good school achievement as measured by school marks, among superior high-school students. The results are summarized in the following paragraphs, and a table of statistical results appears in the Appendix, Table 4-1 and 4-2.

Personal-Social Adjustment. Scores on the California Psychological Inventory were significantly higher for the Achievers among the boys than they were for the Nonachievers. Among the girls the Achievers also had a higher score, but the difference was not statistically significant.

The data on personal-social adjustment from the ninth grade show a consistent pattern. Achievers among boys are characterized by high social-leadership scores and low aggression scores. Among girls, achievers have high leadership scores and low withdrawal scores.

Thus the personal-social adjustment of the Achievers among these youth with superior ability is better than that of the Nonachievers.

Social Class. When the Achievers and Nonachievers were compared on social status, there was no reliable difference between them. This is an important finding, as higher social status is strongly associated with school achievement when the entire group is studied. Among the top third in ability the number of lower-status youth is not large. The lower-class youth who succeed in scoring in the top third on an intelligence test may be those with a considerable achievement drive, who are likely to be fairly well motivated for school achievement.

Educational Motivation Score. The boys and girls in the superior-ability group were interviewed about the topics included in the motivation theory that has just been sketched. Thus, they were asked what adults were especially important to them, whether their best friends were going to college, what school subjects they liked best, how important good grades were to them, how much reading they did and what kind of books they read, and what their occupational goals were. The interview was scored for elements favorable to school achievement. The total scores from the interview showed the Achievers to be substantially higher than the Nonachievers among both sexes. The most striking differences were found in the areas of identification (adults important to the subject who had gone to college or were favorably disposed toward education) and in topics related to intrinsic pleasure in learning, such as reading interests and liking for school subjects.

In this connection there was another kind of evidence available. The mothers of these students were interviewed, and were asked to name the hobbies of their children. These hobbies or special interests were sorted into an "academic" category including such interests as reading, collections, chess, science, maps, writing, and dramatics; and a "nonacademic" category. The Achievers had a much greater number of academic hobbies, more than twice as many as the Nonachievers had. Mothers also indicated their own goals for the children. Mothers of Achievers said they wanted their children to attend college more often (90 per cent to 73 per cent) than did mothers of Nonachievers. Mothers of Achievers also said they wanted their children to earn top grades more frequently than did mothers of Nonachievers.

Need for Achievement. The scores of the McClelland test for unconscious need for achievement showed a tendency for boys and girls who were achievers to score higher than those who were nonachievers. However, the difference between achievers and nonachievers was not statistically significant.

Conclusions

The boys and girls who achieve well in school generally are those who have the advantage of families that help them and stimulate them to do good school work, in addition to their average or superior mental ability. They also get along well with other boys and girls. In this, as in so many other things, the biblical parable of the talents is borne out. "Unto everyone that hath shall be given, and he shall have abundance, but from him that hath not, even that which he hath shall be taken away."

However, educational achievement is not an automatic process that comes out mechanically from a hopper, into which social status, ability, and personal-social adjustment have been thrown together. Motivation for school achievement is necessary, and this comes about through the experience of a child with his family, his friends and neighbors, his teachers, and the world as he senses it directly and through books and pictures. The crude factors of social class, IQ, and social adjustment score merely indicate something of the quality of the child's experience. There are a minority who have the kind of experience that leads to good school achievement in spite of poverty in the home, or average intelligence, or poor social adjustment. It appears that the school may be especially important for this minority, by supplying some of the motivating experience that they do not get at home.

ADOLESCENCE

5

PROGRESS THROUGH SCHOOL

IN THE PRECEDING CHAPTERS the River City children have been brought through the elementary school period and into their adolescence. As they move into their teens, the school becomes more of a test of their equipment for life. Those who are doing well in school begin to use the school as a testing ground for their vocational explorations, and the school becomes more and more *their* world, in which they try out for themselves a variety of adult roles. On the other hand, those who are doing poorly in school find it more and more frustrating or boring, and they look around for alternative ways of growing up; but they do not find good alternatives.

River City is close to the national average in respect to the progress boys and girls make in school. In 1958, when this particular study group reached the usual high-school graduation age, 64 per cent graduated from high school, whereas the national average was 63 per cent. The proportion of boys and girls reaching various levels of the educational ladder are reported in Table 13. Eventually this group will range in education from the seventh grade to the level of a doctor's degree, although the information available at this writing goes only as far as the end of the first year of college.

49

Information is available in Table 13 on 432 out of the 487 boys and girls in the study group, which includes all those who remained in the community until the close of the study as well as many who moved away but could be traced.

The youth of River City can be divided into three roughly equal groups with respect to educational level attained. One-third dropped out of school before reaching high-school graduation; another third ceased their formal education at the end of high school; and a third went beyond high school, most of them to college and a few to nursing school or business school. This final group makes up about 28 per cent in Table 13, but it will be increased in subsequent years

TABLE 13. NUMBERS OF STUDENTS REACHING DIFFERENT LEVELS OF EDUCATION

	Boys	Girls	Total	Per cent of Group
College—successful in first year	43	44	87	20.1
College—dropouts by end of first year	15	3	18	4.2
(Total college)	(58)	(47)	(105)	(24.3)
Nursing or Business school	1	14	15	3.5
High school graduate only	70	90	160	37.0
High school dropouts				
12th grade	14	10	24	5.6
11th grade	25	17	42	9.7
10th grade	14	20	34	7.9
9th grade	27	19	46	10.6
7th & 8th grade	4	2	6	1.4
(Total dropouts)	(84)	(68)	(152)	(35.2)
Total	213	219	432	100
No information	34	21	55	
Total—entire group	247	240	487	

as some boys and a few girls go on to college after a delay of one or more years for military service or for employment.

Sex Differences. More boys than girls dropped out of school, and therefore more girls than boys finished high school. At this point the balance shifted, with more boys than girls going to college. However, more boys than girls failed in the first year of college. Thus girls were much more successful than boys in school, up to the second year of college.

Prediction of Progress through School

What kinds of boys and girls go to college, what kinds stop their formal education with high-school graduation, and what kinds drop out of school before high-school graduation? To what extent is it possible to predict by the age of 11 or 12 how far a particular boy or girl will go in school? These questions will be answered here and in chapter 8.

Table 14 gives the basic data on the relations of intelligence and social status to progress through school. These two factors are

TABLE 14. SOCIAL CLASS AND INTELLIGENCE IN RELA-TION TO PROGRESS THROUGH SCHOOL

	Boys			Girls		
	College and Post HS	HS Grad	HS Dropout	College and Post HS	HS Grad	HS Dropout
Intelligence Quartile						
IV (high)	27	13	4	36	23	3
III	22	17	18	18	24	12
II	7	25	25	3	26	27
I	3	15	37	4	17	26
Social Class						
A	15	4	1	18	2	1
B	27	22	9	22	28	10
C	15	25	38	20	46	23
D	2	19	36	1	14	34
Total	59	70	84	61	90	68

[1] Reprinted with permission from Robert J. Havighurst and Bernice L. Neugarten, *Society and Education*, 2nd Edition. Boston: Allyn and Bacon, Inc., 1962. Table 9.2.

strongly predictive of school progress. The intelligence data come from the tests given in the sixth grade. The IQ scores were divided into quartiles and are reported in Table 14 in relation to the various levels of educational progress attained by the youth of River City. (Tables 5-1 and 5-2 in the Appendix give more detailed information on the interaction of IQ and social class in relation to progress through school.)

There is a close connection between intellectual ability and school progress. In the highest quartile, half of the girls and over half of the boys went to college; less than a tenth dropped out of school before high-school graduation. By contrast, in the lowest quartile less than one-tenth continued their education beyond high school, and three-fourths of the boys and over half of the girls dropped out before high-school graduation.

There is an even closer connection between social class and school progress. Four-fifths of the Class A boys and girls went to college, while only one in twenty dropped out of high school. In the lowest social class, only two in fifty-seven boys went to college, and none of the girls did so.

Because of the close relationships between progress in school and social class and intellectual ability, it is interesting to look at the exceptions. For instance, there were two students of high social status who dropped out of high school, one boy and one girl. Both of these students came from families broken by divorce, both had below-average ability, both did below-average work in school, and both had problems of social and personal adjustment. The girl married while still in school and finally dropped out of school to be with her husband who was in the service. She intends to finish high school when her husband returns to his college education. The boy disliked school and dropped out to go to work.

There were also two students of the lowest social status, Class D, who went to college, both boys. Both boys come from broken homes. One boy has better than average ability, did good work in high school, won a small scholarship to college, and is doing better than average work in college. The other boy is of the lowest quartile in IQ, did poor work in high school but stayed on because of his interest and skill in athletics. He won an athletic scholarship to college but failed in his freshman year because of poor academic work. Both boys have superior personal and social adjustment and have been quite successful in their summer and part-time employment.

There are more exceptions to the rule that high intellectual ability goes with high-school graduation. The seven students in the top quartile of intellectual ability who dropped out of high school were varied in their school records and personal and social adjustment scores. However, they had one thing in common—they all came from homes which deemphasized education. Only one parent out of 14 of this group had finished high school. Most were in social classes B and C.

Of the five students in the lowest quartile of IQ who went to college, three were from homes of high social status and were admitted to small colleges with relatively low standards of admission. Two of them have continued into their sophomore year by dint of effort and social skills. A fourth failed and dropped out of a teachers' college. The fifth of these students is the boy mentioned above who won the athletic scholarship but failed in his freshman year of college.

It is clear that other factors as well as those measured by intelligence tests help to determine how well a boy or girl does in school.

The highest person in IQ stood sixteenth in the class in school marks, whereas a boy who ranked about thirtieth in IQ was tied for the highest rank in school grades.

A fairly typical case is presented by Robert Bregner, who ranked about tenth in the class on intelligence tests, stood twenty-eighth in school marks, and was outstanding in leadership and artistic ability in the sixth grade. He comes from a C-class home, and his parents are helping him as much as possible with his college expenses.

But Roy Coleman, a D-class boy, had the same IQ as Robert Bregner, and stood number 136 in his school marks. He graduated from high school with no interest in further education and is now working at a relatively simple job.

Helen Stover, standing at the ninetieth percentile in IQ, was always a good student and stood twelfth in her class on high school grades. She also displayed artistic talent, and was recognized as a leader. Coming from an upper-middle class family, she decided against going to college, took an office job for a short time, and was married at 19.

On the other hand, Barbara Strong, with the same IQ as Helen, and standing eighteenth in her class, has gone to college, although she comes from a working-class family.

Personal and Social Adjustment. Table 15 contains data on personal and social adjustment in relation to school progress. The California Test of Personality is a group test of personal and social adjustment that falls far short of perfection, as do other self-report tests of this type. Nevertheless, it has been found to be fairly valid as a measure of personal and social adjustment for children below about the eighth grade, when they commence to become defensive about questions concerning their feelings. As the test was given in the sixth grade, it is reasonably valid, although it has a high correlation with socioeconomic status, which makes it suspect for comparing children of contrasting social classes. More than half of those in the top quartile on this test went to college, and only six dropped out of high school. By contrast, almost half of those in the lowest quartile dropped out of school, and only three went to college. There seems to be no consistent pattern among those of high adjustment who dropped out of high school. Some girls dropped out to get

TABLE 15. PROGRESS IN SCHOOL RELATED TO EARLY PREDICTIVE MEASURES

	Dropouts		High School Grad.	Nursing or Bus. School	College Dropout	College Success 1st yr.
	Grades 7–10	11–12				
N =	86	66	160	15	18	87
Social Status						
A (high)	41	0	2	6	2	4	27
B	118	5	11	53	4	7	38
C	167	29	35	68	8	6	21
D (low)	106	52	18	33	1	1	1
Social Leadership						
Q IV	111	3	4	36	6	6	56
Q III	107	8	13	55	5	6	20
Q II	103	22	22	41	3	5	10
Q I	103	47	26	27	1	1	1
No inf.	8	6	1	1	0	0	0
California Test of Personality						
QIV	80	4	2	22	7	5	40
QIII	79	12	14	29	3	4	17
QII	75	11	20	32	0	3	9
QI	78	24	14	36	1	1	2
No inf.	120	35	16	41	4	5	19
Aggressive Maladjustment						
QIV	86	27	22	26	2	4	5
QIII	91	16	19	35	3	1	17
QII	83	10	9	28	4	6	26
QI	92	8	8	40	3	3	30
No inf.	80	25	8	31	3	4	9

married; some boys to go into the armed services, and some to get a job. All but one are having at least average success in what they are doing. All three students who were low on this personality test but went to college had high intellectual ability. One of the three, a boy, dropped out of college after a few months; two girls have stayed in successfully.

The social-leadership scores also predicted progress in school quite well. Those with high social-leadership scores tended to go furthest in school.

The aggressive-maladjustment scores were predictive of school drop-outs. The majority of students who were most aggressive in the sixth grade dropped out of high school, whereas the majority of least aggressive students graduated from high school, many going on to college. This does not mean that those graduating from high school and going on to college lacked initiative and ability to attack a problem aggressively; it does mean that they were not acting in a hostile way toward other boys and girls and toward school and the adult society.

Motivation and Progress through School

Motivation or desire for education and what education implies is a potent factor in determining how far a boy or girl goes in school. Motivation is itself related to ability and social status, but also to other personal qualities and to the nature of the school program. It is these two elements of motivation which will now be discussed.

Ellen. Ellen Forman is a Class A girl of above average intellectual ability. The other girls in her ability and social class category divided about evenly between going to college and stopping with high-school graduation. Ellen had an older boy friend, a serious, hard-working upper-middle class boy of above-average ability, who graduated from high school when Ellen was a sophomore, and went away to college. At Christmas when he came home they decided that it was cruel to stay apart any longer, and they asked their parents for permission to marry. Ellen promised her father that she would eventually finish high school, and then went with her new husband to the university town and commenced keeping house, planning to enter high school the following September. Before that time she was pregnant, and she has not yet gone back to high school.

Such personal motivation factors caused some of the high-status and high-ability boys and girls to terminate their schooling earlier than most others of similar ability and social status.

Henry. On the other hand, there is Henry Stone, a Class-C boy in the lowest quartile of ability. His widowed mother has encouraged him to do as well as possible in school and has maintained a close watch over his behavior and over his associates since he was old enough to be in danger of getting into trouble in the slum neighborhood where they live. During his junior high-school years, Henry came under the influence of the pastor of his church, became active in the youth group in church, and began to devote himself to his studies in school with the idea of becoming a minister. He graduated from high school at about the middle of his class, and is now working his way through a small, church-supported college.

The motivation of a boy or girl for education depends also upon the nature of the school program and the school staff. If the school is an interesting and rewarding place, a boy or girl is likely to stay in school until graduation, and to want further education.

Youth with special nonintellectual talents are likely to have their educational motivations much influenced by the opportunity to develop their special abilities in school. This is seen in River City in the difference in motivation between those with musical talent and those with artistic talent, which was discussed in Chapter 2.

Achievers vs. Nonachievers in Progress through School. The study of achieving and nonachieving boys and girls who were in the upper third of the cohort in IQ has been reported in Chapter 4. This study showed that able boys and girls who achieve in relation to their ability in high school are more likely to go to college than are those who do not achieve up to their ability level. The majority of the Achievers of both sexes made good in college, whereas the majority of the Nonachievers did not go beyond high-school graduation. The results of this study are shown in Table 16.

TABLE 16. EDUCATIONAL CAREERS OF ABLE PUPILS WHO DIFFERED IN HIGH-SCHOOL ACHIEVEMENT

Highest Educational Level	Boys		Girls	
	Achievers	Nonachievers	Achievers	Nonachievers
College success (1st year)	16	7	16	8
College dropout	3	3	1	0
Nursing or Bus. school	0	0	3	3
High school grad	5	12	9	18
High school dropout	0	2	0	0

A STUDY OF HIGH-SCHOOL DROPOUTS

It is clear that progress through school is related to social status, ability, personal and social adjustment, and personal motivation for education. These factors are all interrelated, and therefore it is not possible to say what factors are most truly causes and what ones are results or consequences of these causes.

It is important, though, to recognize the fact that dropping out of school before high-school graduation under present conditions in River City is a sign of general maladjustment to society and is an unfavorable prognosis for the future. Whereas dropping out of school to go to work was a normal thing in 1900, and even as late as 1930 a young person who quit school for a job might be taking a solid step forward toward adulthood, this is seldom the case in 1960.

A special study of dropouts in River City has made this conclusion abundantly clear. This study was planned to include every dropout except the few who completed the twelfth grade but did not get enough credits to win a high-school diploma.

Numbers and Ages of Dropouts

Of 432 students for whom educational career records are complete, 35 per cent (152) did not graduate from high school. There were 138 who dropped out before completing the twelfth grade, and 14 others who finished the grade but did not earn a high-school diploma.

Thirty per cent of the dropouts left school in the first six months after their sixteenth birthday. Forty-six per cent left school after 16½ years of age. This leaves 24 per cent who quit school before the legal school-leaving age of 16. One student dropped out when in the seventh grade, several in the eighth grade, and the largest number when in the ninth grade. About equal numbers dropped out of the tenth, eleventh, and twelfth grades.

Since 24 per cent dropped out before reaching the legal school-leaving age of 16, some explanation for this is needed. This number did not include any who quit school in June but reached their sixteenth birthday before the following September. They were all counted as age 16 on the dropout roll. About two-thirds of the "illegal" dropouts were girls. One of them was 14 when she dropped out due to pregnancy. Several were married before they were 16, and dropped out at the time of marriage, frequently because they were pregnant at the time. The school authorities generally regarded obvious pregnancy as a good reason for dropping out of school, regardless of the age of the girl. One girl moved out of town and did not enter school in the town to which she moved. Another had illness in the family and dropped out in order to help at home. A few said they didn't like school and managed to stay out of sight of the truant officer until they were 16. This was the usual history of the boys who dropped out before age 16. These boys were generally in so much trouble at school that the school authorities tacitly accepted the fact that the boys were not in school. None of the early dropout boys was married during the first year out of school, and only 6 of 13 boys found a steady job. Nine of them had been arrested for various degrees of delinquency.

Table 5-2 (Appendix) shows the social class and intelligence quartiles of the dropouts in relation to the age of dropping out. Table 14 compares the dropouts with the stayin population in social class and intelligence. Forty per cent of the dropouts came from the lowest quartile of intelligence, as against 13 per cent of the stayins. However, there were 6 per cent of dropouts from the top quartile of intelligence.

Social class differences are evident in Table 5-2. Forty-six per cent of the dropouts came from Class D, compared with 13 per cent of the stayins.

It is clear that low intelligence and low socioeconomic status are important factors in dropping out of school, but it is also clear that these factors alone are not adequate explanations. For instance, although some 70 students of Class D dropped out of school, yet about 40 did stay in school until high-school graduation. Most of the Class A and B students finished high school, but one in seven dropped out. Consequently additional factors that influence dropping out of school were sought by comparing the dropouts with a control group matched as far as possible for intelligence and social class.

Since it was known that dropping out of school was associated with below average intelligence and social status, it would not be useful to compare dropouts with those who stayed in school unless these particular factors could be kept constant. That is, a comparison group of boys and girls who stayed in school was needed, and it was important that this comparison group have the same socioeconomic status and intelligence as the dropout group. However, it is not easy to find as many boys and girls of lower socioeconomic status and lower mental ability who stay in school as the number who drop out.

There were 138 dropouts; that is, boys and girls who quit school before completing the twelfth grade. The ideal comparison group would have been a group of equal size in which for every dropout there was a boy or girl of the same sex, quartile in IQ, and social class. Thus the two groups, dropouts and control stayins, would consist of matched pairs. A total of 85 boys and girls were found who could match 85 dropouts on these factors. Beyond that some more were added who matched the remaining dropouts on sex and *either* intelligence or social class, but not both. Eventually the control group consisted of 127 people of whom 111 were matched with dropouts for IQ, 101 for social class, with 85 appearing in both the IQ control and the social-class control groups. Comparisons could then be made between dropouts and the total control group of 127, or one or the other of the two partial control groups.

Comparisons of Dropouts with Their Control Group

The dropouts have been compared with their control group in five areas of experience: personal-social adjustment, attitudes and values, finances, school experiences, and area of residence. These comparisons were based on data in the files of the study and on information determined from an interview made four to six months after the dropout had left school, and parallel interviews with the members of the control group.

Personal-social Adjustment. It will be remembered that the California Test of Personality, given in the sixth grade, showed that those who stayed longer in school had higher scores. But when the dropouts are compared with the control group of the same social class and intelligence, this difference largely disappears. At the sixth grade, there is not a reliable difference between the two groups. However, at the tenth grade the stayins were reliably higher than the dropouts on the California Psychological Inventory, which is designed to measure personal-social adjustment in an indirect manner. This difference was present in spite of the fact that the earliest and more maladjusted half of the dropouts were not in school and did not take this test.

Attitudes and Values with Respect to Education and Work. In the interviews the boys and girls were asked why they dropped out or stayed in school, as the case might be. The dropouts give the following major reasons:

Negative experiences and negative attitudes in school—47 per cent

Poor social adjustment—18 per cent

Preference or need for work—16 per cent

Marriage with or without pregnancy—9 per cent

In contrast, the control group gave the following reasons for wanting to stay in school:

Education is needed for getting a job or getting into college—50 per cent

Education is valued for itself—30 per cent

Parental guidance or pressure—13 per cent

Apparently the control group of stayins was more concerned about holding a job and making a vocational success, and they saw education as a means to this end. The control group also showed more positive attitudes to work through their work records. Eighty per cent of controls and 40 per cent of dropouts held part-time jobs while they were in school. Of the controls, 40 per cent had held their jobs for more than a year, whereas only 2 per cent of dropouts had held jobs that long while still in school. The dropouts apparently had ill-defined goals for themselves, or wanted to achieve these goals without effort. But their experience after dropping out of school was generally disappointing. Despite speaking to an interviewer who was markedly permissive, and to whom they frequently expressed great hostility toward school, 56 per cent said they wished they had stayed in school.

Parental attitudes were also involved in the distinction between dropouts and control-group members. The boy or girl was asked how his parents felt about his dropping out or staying in school. The interview generally took place in the home, and the interviewer could often obtain this information directly from a parent. Of the control group, 68 per cent of the parents strongly insisted that their children remain in school. Among the dropouts only 13 per cent of the parents opposed their dropping out. Thirty-four per cent of the dropouts reported their parents to be indifferent about school; only 7 per cent of the controls indicated parental indifference. Six per cent of the dropouts actually were urged to drop out of school by their parents.

Financial Factors. When the dropouts were interviewed six months or more after they had dropped out of school, only 5 per cent gave clear evidence of having to leave school for financial reasons. Seventy-five per cent of them stated quite clearly that there was no financial necessity for leaving school. Furthermore, it was possible to compare the dropouts with their socioeconomic controls who were still in school on the extent to which they contributed to their own support through jobs, payment for board and room, clothing purchases, and the like. When the two groups were compared on these items, it was found that 70 per cent of the controls were mainly self-supporting, whereas 55 per cent of the dropouts were mainly self-supporting.

The two groups could also be compared on ownership of an automobile. At the time of the interview 26 per cent of dropouts and 11 per cent of controls owned cars. It seems that the dropouts were less thrifty and industrious than the controls, although they had much more time free for earning money.

School Experiences. By any criterion that is used the dropouts had less successful, more frustrating experiences in their school lives. Their difficulties at school began in the first and second grade and continued throughout their school careers. In either the academic or the extra curricular fields the story is the same.

For example, there were four times more dropouts than controls retarded at least one year in school. None of the controls failed of promotion after the fifth grade, while some dropouts have failed each year. In elementary school 4 per cent of the dropouts were in the upper third of their classes in school marks against 19 per cent of the controls; this was just reversed in the lowest third of the class marks. In high school the dropouts again made much poorer grades. None of the dropouts was in the upper quartile of the class in grade-point average; 18 per cent of the controls scored in the top quarter. Of the dropouts, 70 per cent were in the lowest quarter against 8 per cent of the controls. Half of all the grades made by the dropouts in high school were D's and F's (failing grades), and only one per cent were A's; the A's were almost all in music and physical education. In reading-achievement scores the controls were consistently higher at every grade level. Table 17 shows that both dropouts and controls improved somewhat in their reading scores through the fourth grade, but then both dropped sharply at the seventh grade. This apparent change may be an artifact of the tests that were used.

Attendance at school is an indicator of general adjustment to school. From kindergarten through seventh grade the dropouts were absent about 20 per cent more than their controls. Then, in

the eighth and ninth grades the absences of the future dropouts
increased rapidly while the absences of controls decreased sharply.
The future dropouts were absent an average of 22 days during the
eighth and ninth grades; their controls were absent an average of
8.5 days. It seems clear that the future dropouts were already dropping out "in their own minds" a couple of years before they dropped
out physically.

Dropouts were equally unsuccessful in extracurricular activities.
Only one dropout held any school government office, and controls

TABLE 17. COMPARISON OF DROPOUTS AND CONTROLS ON READING ACHIEVEMENT

Per cent of pupils	1st Grade			4th Grade			7th Grade		
	Drop Out	Intell. Control	Soc. Class Control	Drop Out	Intell. Control	Soc. Class Control	Drop Out	Intell. Control	Soc. Class Control
Reading scores at or above grade level	40	50	53	56	67	73	20	36	53
Reading scores below grade level	60	50	47	44	33	27	80	64	47

were about twice as active as dropouts in all activities. The major
participation of dropouts was in attending athletic events and dances.
These experiences led 67 per cent of the dropouts to express strong
dislike for school as did 12 per cent of the controls. The majority
of the dropouts were thus finding school to be a very frustrating
place which they would like to avoid as much as possible.

Some attitudes toward extracurricular activities are shown in the
following excerpts from interviews with dropouts.

"Were you interested in the Girls Athletic Association or the Y Teen
group?"
"No, I wasn't."
Sister: "She went down to the Y.M. for swimming."
"What did you think of the social life at junior high school, did you care
at all for the dances?"
"I didn't know that they had them."
"Did you go to any of the games?"
"No."
"Do you feel that you were generally a part of the junior high school as
far as the activities were concerned?"

"No, I don't.   I went to one dance and stayed for ten minutes.   I never went to another one."

"Do you feel like you were happy in junior high school?"

She laughed.   "Just before school started and after school was out."

In spite of their frustrations in school, the experience of a few months out of school made many of the dropouts doubt the wisdom of their "decision."   They were asked, "Is it better out of school or in school?"   "If you had it to do over, would you go on or drop out?"   The quotations that follow give something of the doubt and uncertainty of these young people.

No.   I wasn't expecting to quit when I was sixteen.   I was just not getting along well out there and then they wrote that note home.   I think that if I had been getting along better, I would have kept on going to school. I don't know though.   I like the job a lot better.   I have had this same job since I left school. . . .   I don't know.   It would have been all right to go on in school if things were going all right.   But if things weren't going al right I suppose I would quit again.   If I'd been successful in school I would have stayed on."

"It just seemed to me that all the other kids were out playing while I was in school.   They said to me, 'Stay in.'   I said, 'You found out the hard way, let me find out the hard way.   Let me find out for myself.'   It's the same way about getting married.   I always say, 'Let me get married and find out the hard way if it's no good . . . '"

"I couldn't get along with teachers.   That was the main reason.   I really didn't like any of them . . . .   In a way it seems better (being out of school) and in a way it don't.   When you are in school, at least you have some place to go and pass the time."

"If I had it to do over again, I am sure I would go on."

"Why do you say that?"

"Well, really, I was thinking about the vacation I would have here but I find it really is not a vacation.   It is a lot of work keeping a house." Here she shook her head and continued.   "And when the baby comes, it will be a lot more.   One baby is all I want."

Residential Area.   A family of low social status generally lives in an area of similar families, but occasionally such a family lives in a neighborhood where the families are generally of higher status, and the children therefore attend a school with children of generally higher status.   In this situation, the children may tend to follow the educational values of the neighborhood and to stay in school.

Table 5-3 (Appendix) shows how the dropouts and their social class controls compare in the areas where they lived in and the schools they attended.   There is a tendency for dropouts to live in the lower social class areas, whereas their socioeconomic controls live in areas with more middle-class neighbors.

CONCLUSIONS

School provides the only pathway to adolescence in River City, and high school is the only easily travelled route through adolescence to adulthood. For the third of River City youth who do not finish high school the way to adulthood is not an easy one. We see in later chapters that the dropouts have the greatest difficulty in growing up successfully. They are the most vulnerable to delinquency. They get the poorest jobs, if they get jobs at all. They have the most trouble with marriage. The churches see very little of them.

These boys and girls are somehow alien to the society in which they are trying to live. The evidence is clear that they start school with cultural handicaps, they have inadequate help and encouragement from their parents, and they accumulate a record of failure and frustration in school which drives them out of school at the earliest possible date. Early failure in school starts a process of alienation from society that leads them into delinquency and other forms of adolescent maladjustment.

With its present type of program, the school serves these children poorly. As late as a generation ago this group had the alternative of juvenile work leading to adult competence. Now this alternate pathway has narrowed and seems to be disappearing. The school is challenged to create a new and more satisfactory way to adulthood for a third of our youth.

In contrast to the dropouts we find another third of River City youth moving through high school and on to college and other post-high-school institutions with relative success. For them the educational system is working well.

As early as the sixth grade it is possible to discover the probable dropouts with considerable accuracy, and also to discover those who will go farthest in school. If these subgroups are recognized and treated wisely it should be possible to make the school system into a more effective institution for helping the various types of children to grow up successfully.

6

~~~~

DELINQUENCY—DEAD END
STREET

B OYS AND GIRLS normally grow up by way of the
school into adolescence in a fairly smooth way. As
we have seen in the preceding chapter their success in school is related
to their intelligence, their personality, and their family background.

But there is a substantial and worrisome minority who do not grow
up successfully. Their failure to master the tasks of growing through
middle childhood becomes more and more evident to them, their age-
mates, their teachers and their parents. Usually the first sign of
trouble is failure in school—and often failure to learn to read with
ease and as a matter of course. Almost always there is a disturbance
of the child's social adjustment which is noted by teachers and by
age-mates, either as aggressiveness or as withdrawal.

By the age of 12 or 13, this child generally shows signs of personal-
social maladjustment and also is doing poor work in school. This
combination is a dangerous one. It is found in about 15 per cent of
children, and is a pretty sure indicator of trouble ahead. Another
group of about equal size either shows failure in school or personal-
social maladjustment, but not both at once. This group is likely to
have some trouble in growing up, but not as much as the group that
combines school failure and personal-social maladjustment.

Difficulty in growing up is met by a boy or girl at first with efforts
to overcome or to get around the difficulty. He may work harder at

his school work, and this may prove successful. Or he may find some alternative pathway of growth outside of the school, such as a job. He may find some substitutes for growing up that look and feel like the real thing, for a time. Or he may seek excitement and pleasure through which he can forget his failure. Finally, he may give up the attempt to grow up, and either accept a hopeless and helpless inferiority or discover a world of day dreams in which he can imagine himself to be successful.

All of these reactions to growth failure can be seen among River City youth. Boys tend to make more active and strenuous efforts, and their activities sometimes become so aggressive that the boys are labelled delinquents. Girls tend more toward the passive forms of behavior, and thus are not seen so often as delinquent. But there are some active, aggressive delinquent girls and there are passive, withdrawn, and intimidated boys.

Some 30 to 40 per cent of youth quit school without graduating from high school, the majority of them near their sixteenth birthday, when it becomes legal to leave school. This means that they must seek some other pathway of growth than the school. Some of them find work, and grow with their growing mastery of work attitudes and skills. Many of the girls do not find work, but they marry at ages 15 or 16 or 17, and thus become wives and mothers while still in their adolescence.

Largely within this group of school dropouts are found the boys and girls who suffer most seriously from failure to grow up successfully. Most of the juvenile delinquents are in this group. Also a number of shy and inferior boys and girls with weak personalities are to be found here.

Altogether, some 15 per cent of a typical youth population are in this failure group. The size of this group is larger in the slum area of a big city, and much smaller in an upper-middle class suburb. The number, 15 per cent, is not inevitable or irreducible. It depends on how well the boys and girls of a community are treated in home, school, and community.

Causes and Types of Delinquency

Delinquent or law-breaking behavior by young people under 18 is called juvenile delinquency. The various forms of delinquency can be grouped under three categories:

1. *Delinquency due to severe personality disturbance.* In this category there are two types of delinquency. One consists of ex-

tremely aggressive and uncontrolled behavior, and may include murder. Children of this type have little or no inner moral control, and have generally been brought up by a parent or parents who neglected them and failed both to love and to punish them with consistency. This is sometimes called the "psycopathic personality." It is rare, and there was no clear-cut example of it in the River City group.

The other type of personality disturbance consists of a severe and pervasive anxiety which makes the child do strange things. In contrast to the disturbance previously described, this child is over-inhibited and suffers from pangs of conscience or fits of anxiety for mild sins and even for imagined misbehavior. Conscious or unconscious feelings of guilt cause this child to commit acts for which he is almost sure to be found out and punished, such as setting fires and compulsive stealing. There was one probable case of this kind, in the study group. This was a boy who was frequently arrested for speeding and other traffic violations. The case of Rex, described later in this chapter, also shows some of the elements of neurotic guilt.

Since emotional disturbance is not something which is either present or not present in a person, but is present to some degree in all people at one time or another, it is difficult to distinguish this form of delinquency from others. Probably the cases are rather rare in which the juvenile delinquent suffers from a really severe emotional disturbance.

2. *Delinquency that is a normal part of adolescent development.* Sometimes called "developmental" delinquency, this is a kind of behavior related to the crises and conflicts of adolescence, and the person outgrows it. Most adolescents do some mild stealing or destroy some property, but they do not do this often, and they are seldom caught. When they are older, they look back on this behavior with mild feelings of guilt or with mild amusement, and wonder why they did such irrational things. If they are caught, they are seldom brought to court and are usually let off with a warning by the police or by the persons whom they have offended. This delinquency does not figure heavily in the official statistics. The dividing lines between this and the other two types of delinquency are hazy ones. Thinking in terms of growth failure, one might say that developmental delinquency is an incident that disturbs but does not prevent growth to adulthood, whereas the following form is a real obstacle to satisfactory growth.

3. *Delinquency that originates in maladjustments in the social structure.* The most common type of juvenile delinquency in the

United States and other industrialized societies is a social phenomenon carried on by a subgroup of youth who are "at odds" with the greater society in which they live. In a sense, they are at war with society. They are alienated from it; they do not wish to obey its rules.

This group of boys and girls have failed in their efforts to grow up by playing the game according to the rules of society, which means doing satisfactory work in school, or getting a steady job, and getting along well with the great body of their age-mates. As a result of this failure, they seek illegal and socially undesirable substitutes for growth. These illegal and socially undesirable forms of behavior are lumped together under the title of juvenile delinquency, and they have the common features of leading nowhere, as far as the task of growing up is concerned.

Delinquency of this type is often carried on by gangs of youth, the gang serving to give backing to the stand of the youth against the greater society, creating a kind of "delinquent subculture" that supports delinquent behavior and recruits new members as youngsters grow into adolescence. Many of the boys and girls who are delinquent in this way are fairly normal in their personal and social adjustment within their own social groups. They grow up in neighborhoods and in families where drunkenness is common; where fighting is a frequent thing, and a boy must be ready to fight in order to protect himself from others; where sexual promiscuity is visible, and many girls see their mothers or sisters so engaged; where successful stealing is condoned. Such children will have a strong likelihood of becoming delinquent.

At least half of juvenile delinquents come from families in the lowest economic quarter of the population. They tend to live in the slums, or demoralized areas of the great cities, though they may also be found in every town or rural country. Thus juvenile delinquency is statistically a lower-class phenomenon, although three-fourths of lower-class youth do not become delinquents.

Their numbers have increased greatly since the close of the Second World War. During the decade from 1948 to 1958 the annual number of juvenile court cases doubled in the United States, while the juvenile population, aged 10 to 18, was increasing 27 per cent.

Juvenile Delinquency in River City

Although River City has not experienced the extreme forms of juvenile delinquency—murder, rape, and drug addiction—that have caused consternation in the metropolitan areas during recent years, there is nevertheless a substantial amount of juvenile crime.

The over-all crime rate of River City, adult and juvenile, is about 10 per cent below the national average, and quite similar to that of other medium-sized cities in the Midwest region.

A considerable number of children come into contact with police. From the group of 247 boys, a total of 96 had some contact with the police between 1950 and the middle of 1959 when the records for juvenile delinquency were closed. At this time most of the group were 18 or 19 years old. Also recorded in some form of delinquent behavior were 18 out of 240 girls.

It is much too loose a definition of delinquency, however, to call all of these boys and girls juvenile delinquents. Of the 114 offenders more than 40 have had only one contact with the police, and these were for such minor offenses as truancy, speeding, faulty automobile brakes, breaking windows or street lights. These incidents were simply noted by the police but never became a matter of court record. For example, a woman might observe some 10-year-old neighbor boys shooting at birds with an air rifle and call the police, who would come out, take the boys to their mothers, and warn them against playing with these weapons. The police would make a note of this, and thus a boy might get on our list, even though he never came into contact with the police again.

Another third of the group have had more than a single contact with the police, but the reasons for the contact were definitely of minor seriousness.

In order to get a more accurate knowledge of the nature and extent of juvenile delinquency in the River City group, a rating was made for each contact a person had with the police. The ratings varied from 1 to 4 for seriousness of the offense, and from 1 to 4 for the disposition of the case—whether the individual was let off with a warning, was brought into court, declared delinquent, fined, put in prison, sent to the state reformatory, and so on. The total delinquency scores ranged from 2 to 35.

These delinquency records were then classified in four categories. There were 46 boys and 11 girls in the least serious category, IV, with scores below 5. Another 16 boys and 5 girls were in category III, with scores from 5 to 8. Most of these cases consisted of two contacts with the police, for relatively slight offenses. Categories II and I contained 18 and 16 boys respectively, and one girl in each category. These were definitely more serious. Category I was serious enough to suggest that there was real danger of a criminal career.

We will speak of those in categories I, II, and III as "delinquents" although some of them are not delinquent by the usual legal definition. Nevertheless, they have done things that, if continued as they grow older, will result in arrest and punishment. Two examples of Category I cases are given in the following paragraphs.

Rex. Rex was a boy of low mentality (IQ 77) who hated school and was frequently truant. His father was a steady worker but would frequently get angry with the boy and beat him. At the age of thirteen the boy was picked up by the police and admitted stealing $20 from the pocketbook of a lady in a store. His mother repaid the money and no charges were pressed. At fourteen he was arrested for an attempted breakin at a filling station. He was later declared delinquent by the county court, placed in a detention home, and later transferred to a foster home for a short period. He was given a medical examination but no pathology was found. At eighteen he was picked up several times for drunkenness, fined several times, and finally jailed. He is fast becoming an habitual drunkard. This is a case of emotional maladjustment abetted by a delinquent subculture.

Sue. Sue was first picked up at the age of fifteen for hanging around downtown with a group of girls. A month later she was reported to the police by her father for being truant, not coming home nights, and being unmanageable. She was married at sixteen but was reported to the police shortly afterward by her neighbors who complained of the filthiness of the apartment and the neglect of her small baby. The police found her at that time in a tavern. Two months later she was brought in for soliciting men in a tavern. She continues to live with her parents and to practice prostitution.

Altogether 50 River City boys are in delinquency categories I, II, or III, or slightly over 20 per cent of the age-group. At least categories I and II, and some of category III, would be included in the national delinquency reports. This proportion may be compared with the estimates made by the U.S. Childrens Bureau that as of 1958 approximately 20 per cent of boys in the United States were being brought into court on delinquency charges one or more times while they were aged 10 to 18.

The ratio of delinquent boys to delinquent girls in the River City cohort was 7 to 1, there being seven girls in categories I, II, and III. This ratio on a nationwide basis is generally given as 5 to 1 or 4 to 1.

Table 18 shows how delinquency is related to social class in this group. Out of 68 D-class boys, 23 are in the three more serious categories, together with 5 out of 58 D-class girls. Delinquency as it has been identified here tends to be concentrated in the working class, and particularly in the lower part of the working class.

TABLE 18. DELINQUENCY AND SOCIAL CLASS IN RIVER CITY[1]

	Delinquency Category				
	Most Serious			Least Serious	Total No. in
	I	II	III	IV	Age Cohort
Social Class	*Boys*				
A (Upper & upper-middle)	0	1	0	2	22
B (Lower-middle)	2	2	4	14	64
C (Upper-lower)	5	6	7	19	91
D (Lower-lower)	9	9	5	11	70
Total	16	18	16	46	247
	Girls				
A	0	0	0	0	21
B	0	0	0	0	65
C	0	1	0	6	94
D	1	0	4	5	58
Total	1	1	5	11	238

[1] Reprinted with permission from Robert J. Havighurst and Bernice L. Neugarten, *Society and Education*, 2nd Edition. Boston: Allyn and Bacon, Inc. 1962. Table 14.1.

All of those in category I, the most serious, dropped out of school without finishing high school. Fifteen of 19 in category II, and 18 of 21 in category III also dropped out of school.

In category I, only one-third of the group have grown up with both parents actually in the home. Intellectually, most of the group are in the lowest quarter, and only 3 out of 17 are above average. However, the less serious categories of delinquency are not so strictly related to intelligence.

Thus it can be seen that delinquency is concentrated among those of lower socioeconomic status, who drop out of school, who have relatively low intelligence, and who come from broken and inadequate homes.

However, a larger number of boys and girls who have grown up with similar disadvantages do not become delinquent. This fact must be explained by any acceptable theory of the causes of juvenile delinquency.

The following theory of delinquency causation may have some validity for River City. This theory holds that boys and girls will attempt to succeed according to the usual standards prevailing in the community and supported by their teachers and also by their parents, though not always completely by the latter. However, if they are unable to achieve success by legitimate means they are likely to turn to delinquency.

The majority, even of Class D boys and girls, succeed reasonably well, at least by their own standards. They get along in school, and a considerable group graduate from high school. The boys get work when they finish school. Many of the girls get married almost as soon as they finish or quit school.

However, a substantial subgroup, consisting mainly of lower-class youth, and especially of boys of the lower-lower class, do not find success in these ways. In this subgroup most of the boys and girls are failing in school, and they experience the repeated frustration of being talked about by teachers and by classmates as "dummies." This frustration begins to be felt keenly by the fifth or sixth grade, when teachers begin to grade pupils more realistically. The frustration culminates in the junior high school, when all the boys and girls from all the elementary schools come together. Here the competition for school grades becomes keener. A boy who was "getting by" in a slum elementary school has more difficulty in the junior high school.

At the same time, some of the lower-class children feel that they are the objects of social discrimination in the school. Coming from the "wrong side of the tracks," they feel, or are made to feel, ill at ease at the parties and dances of the junior high school. In our interviews with delinquent youngsters we heard a great deal of bitterness and resentment expressed against the middle and upper-class children who "think they are something" and wear better clothes and make fun of the lower-class boys and girls. Generally the members of this delinquent or predelinquent subgroup quit going to school social affairs after one or two trials, and dropped out of school social life before they dropped out of academic life. They turned to disreputable places and doubtful "hang-outs" where they felt more welcome, or to youth centers where the supervisors make a definite effort to make them feel at home, and where they and their friends could set the styles of dancing, clothing, haircuts.

Furthermore, the boys of this group have great difficulty in finding and keeping jobs—either part-time jobs while at school, or full-time jobs after dropping out of school.

Thus this particular subgroup of youth experiences a great deal of frustration or of blockage of the pathway of growing up, both in school and outside of school. It is important to note, however, that this subgroup is a minority of working-class youth. The majority succeed well enough in school and community to stay out of trouble, and some succeed very well indeed.

When success is not achieved by legitimate means adolescent boys and girls are likely to turn to illegitimate activities. There are three possible general patterns of illegitimate or delinquent behavior; the particular pattern a person follows is governed by the opportunities available to him as well as by his own personal makeup.

One pattern is that of crime, especially theft. This will be adopted if there are criminals in the community to set an example to younger people, and if there are ways of using or disposing of stolen goods. In River City there is enough adult crime, and it is well enough organized to make this pattern accessible to youth. It is the dominant delinquency pattern.

A second pattern is that of fighting, especially between gangs. This gives excitement, a certain kind of prestige, and the feeling of group solidarity and mutual support which adolescents want. The opportunity for this pattern is limited in River City, partly because the community is not large enough to permit the development of rival gangs of any size and partly because the police have been on the lookout for incipient gang fighting and have clamped down on anything that seemed to be a start of it. Thus, although there is a considerable amount of individual fighting in River City, usually associated with drunkenness, no organized gang warfare has developed.

The police have been especially vigilant against gang fighting recently, perhaps because of the publicity attached to this phenomenon when it has occurred in some larger cities. For instance, the River City police and newspaper took serious notice of one fight incident recently which they might have ignored if the climate of opinion had been different. This was a situation in which one seventeen-year-old boy accompanied by a couple of friends attacked another boy who was coming out of a movie theater in company with a sixteen-year-old girl who was the wife of the first boy. The boy who was attacked reappeared shortly afterward with some friends, and at this point the police intervened and arrested everybody who seemed to be involved. The incident was reported in detail and with seriousness by the newspaper, and the boys involved in the fighting were given a severe lecture and a warning by the court.

In the larger city with organized juvenile gangs, there is a good deal of fighting over girls, which may lead to shooting and knifing. Knowing this, the River City police may have decided to nip this particular incident in the bud.

A third pattern of delinquency is retreat into some form of passive substitute for success, such as drug-addiction. This comes when the other methods fail, and again depends to some extent upon the personal makeup of a boy or girl. In River City there is little access to drugs, and consequently this pattern is limited to obsessive drinking. Rex, mentioned earlier in the chapter, is probably one of this type. He has tried some stealing, but he is not aggressive enough and not smart enough to "get away" with this and thus to gain esteem from his peers. Consequently he is turning into an alcoholic.

The Prediction of Delinquency

Always a major concern about delinquency is its prevention, and a preventive program usually requires some method of identifying those who are most likely to become delinquent. With this study group we were interested in discovering and testing a method to predict delinquency.

Such a method was worked out and applied to the River City group when they were in the sixth and seventh grades. This consisted of using two instruments to pick out the boys and girls who were most aggressive—that is, who were most likely to fight, bully, steal, break rules, and be truant from school. It was assumed that these boys and girls were most likely to become delinquent later on. The two instruments—the Behavior Description Chart and the Who Are They? Test—are described in the Appendix.

The scores obtained from teachers and from peers were averaged over two years, the sixth and seventh grades, to give a single score for aggressive maladjustment, and this was taken as a prediction of delinquency. There were about 400 pupils for whom these scores were available. (Some who moved into the community after 1953 are not included in this number, and those who were in the special class for the educable mentally handicapped are not included).

The delinquency-prediction scores were then compared with the record of delinquency through 1959, and the results are given in Table 19. Of the 16 boys in delinquency category I (most serious)

6 were in the top 5 per cent of aggressive-maladjustment scores, one was in the second 5 per cent, and 6 were between the percentiles 90 and 75. There were no scores for the other 3 boys. One was in a special class for the mentally handicapped, and the other two moved into River City shortly after the predictive data were obtained.

For categories II and III of delinquency, there was also a strong tendency for the boys to appear in the top quarter on the aggressive maladjustment scores. Thus it appears that the boys who become delinquent have a strong likelihood of getting high scores for aggressive maladjustment.

TABLE 19. RELATION BETWEEN AGGRESSIVE MALADJUSTMENT AND DELINQUENCY AMONG BOYS IN RIVER CITY

Category of Delinquency	Numbers of boys with: Percentile Score for Maladjustment in 6th Grade of School					
	96–100	91–95	76–90	−75	No Data	Total
I Most serious	6	1	6	0	3	16
II	4	2	4	8	0	18
III	5	3	1	7	0	16
Total delinquent	15	6	11	15	3	50
Not delinquent	3	9	28	122	30	192

Looking next at the people who scored in the top 5 per cent on aggressive maladjustment, 20 in all, it is seen that 15 boys were in categories I, II, or III of delinquency, leaving 3 nondelinquent boys and 2 girls, one of whom was delinquent. Looking at the next 5 per cent in aggressive maladjustment, 6 boys were in categories I, II, or III of delinquency, and 9 were not delinquent, leaving 5 girls.

Thus, if the results of this study can be generalized to other similar situations, we can say that boys who score in the top 5 per cent on aggressive maladjustment have a very strong probability of becoming delinquent, and boys who become delinquent have a very strong probability of scoring in the top quarter on aggressive maladjustment.

If this method had been used to screen out predelinquent boys for special preventive help, almost all of the most seriously delinquent boys would have been discovered, but about half of the boys who were destined to appear in categories II and III would have been· overlooked.

If the top 17 per cent of the boys, measured by aggressive maladjustment scores, had been screened out for preventive treatment, we would have secured 21 boys destined to become delinquent and 13 more who were not destined to become delinquent.

If we add to a record of aggressive maladjustment a record of school failure, we can do an even better job of predicting delinquency among boys. For instance, taking the above-mentioned 34 boys with highest aggressive-maladjustment scores and looking at their school records for the fifth, sixth and seventh grades, we find that 20 of the 21 delinquent boys had failing school marks in one or more of the three grades, while 8 of the 13 who did not become delinquent had failing grades.

Thus, by combining the score on aggressive maladjustment with the school record we would have selected 28 boys, of whom 20 were destined to become delinquent and 8 others were not.

If we were to use a simple and economical procedure such as the one just described to screen out the future delinquents we would still miss a third to a half of them because their scores on aggressive maladjustment would not be high enough. We could pick out two-thirds of the future delinquents if we took the top quarter in agressive maladjustment, but then, as is seen in Table 19, we would also have selected a large group of boys not destined to become delinquent.

This procedure, then, would have a great deal of practical value but it could not produce for us all or nearly all of the boys most likely to become delinquent. Furthermore, we should recognize the fact that the combined use of aggressive-maladjustment score and school failure record would occasionally predict wrongly, and for this reason, the screening procedure described above might well be supplemented by a further, second-level study of those screened out by the first-level procedure.

A clue to such a supplemental method has been given by Sheldon and Eleanor Glueck in their study of delinquent boys in the Boston area. They found a number of factors in the family life of the boys they studied that discriminated between the boys who became delinquent and their neighbors who did not become delinquent, although they came from the same social class and neighborhood backgrounds. These qualities of family life have been made into a Delinquency Prediction Scale, which is referred to in Table 20.*

* Details of the Prediction Scale are given in Sheldon and Eleanor Glueck, *Unraveling Juvenile Delinquency*. New York: Commonwealth Fund, 1950. Ch. 20. For a report of the validation of this scale, see Sheldon Glueck, ed., *The Problem of Delinquency*. Boston: Houghton Mifflin, 1959. "New York City Youth Board Validation." pp. 1032–1051.

The Delinquency Prediction Scale requires a visit by an experienced interviewer or social worker to the home to get an interview with the mother or the father. This is expensive, but it might be used economically as a means of studying the small number of families whose sons were screened out by a less costly first-order process, such as the one we have used.

Accordingly, we interviewed the parents of a number of the boys who had high aggressive-maladjustment scores. Some of this interviewing was done when the boys were in seventh or eighth grade, and had not yet had much opportunity to show whether they were to become delinquent. Ideally, it should all have been done at this time, but some was postponed until the boys dropped out of school, at about age 16. Nevertheless, the interview gives a fairly good basis for judging the quality of family relations both as they were when the interview was conducted and as they were when the boy was younger.

The interviewer was instructed to explore the attitudes of father and mother toward the boy, the quality of their supervision of him, and the degree of cohesiveness in the family. Ratings were then made on the basis of the interview, and a prediction was made concerning the possible delinquency of the boy. The Gluecks calculated a delinquency prediction score for each possible rating on five qualities of family life and found, for example, that in their study the chances of delinquency were 86 in 100 for boys with a score of 300–349, and 16 in 100 for boys with scores of 150–199.

Two Cases for the Reader to Try

There follow accounts of the home interviews for two boys both very high in aggressive-maladjustment scores. Both boys had failing marks in school when they were in the fifth to seventh grades. On the basis of this information, it would be predicted that both boys would become delinquent. Yet one boy became delinquent at category II, and the other one did not have any contact with the police. The reader may try to rate the two boys on the quality of their home backgrounds, or at least to decide which one of them has the better and which the worse home, from the point of view of delinquency causation.

Home Visit—DeWayne Fastelle. This interview was made with Mrs. Bond, the mother of DeWayne, when the latter was 15 years old and in the ninth grade of school. Though his measured intelligence was only slightly below average, DeWayne did below-average work in the elementary school, and spent two years in the sixth grade. He was regarded by his age-mates and by his teachers as a highly aggressive boy, according to sociometric tests given when he was in the sixth, seventh, and ninth grades. His sixth grade teacher checked the following adjectives as descriptive of him: aggressive, alert, boastful, bossy, cruel, depressed, honest, loyal, revengeful, show-off, tease, touchy, vindictive.

As he grew older he became more actively aggressive in school, until in the ninth grade he was being sent out of one class after another. Finally, shortly after he reached his sixteenth birthday, he decided to quit school. One of his best friends had just been expelled, and another one had dropped out.

When asked by an interviewer how it seemed to him after he had been out of school several months, DeWayne said: "I'd rather be in. But when I quit I had a feeling that they were going to kick me out anyway. It was quit or get kicked out because of my bad behavior. I couldn't mind my teachers or they couldn't mind me; I don't know which. Anyway, I had mostly study halls when I quit. They had kicked me out of science and social studies and algebra."

Report of Home Visit when DeWayne was just starting ninth grade:

The home is built right up to the old brick sidewalk, with a porch across the front of the old brick structure. The four porch pillars are almost completely rotted away. The Fastelles have four rooms on the second floor, reached by a dirty, dimly lit stairway going up from the back yard. Several strands of clothesline run in a haphazard manner across the littered yard.

As I walked up the stairs I heard footfalls and a door closing, and I saw two forms passing the door, which had three-fourths of an inch clearance underneath. When I knocked there was no answer. When I knocked the second time someone crossed behind the door quickly. A third knock brought DeWayne to the door. I asked if I could see his mother and he invited me in and called his mother, who was in the bedroom straightening up. Noticed in the bedroom were two iron beds and a canvas cot with a few blankets rumpled up on it. The older son, Dale, was asleep face down on another bed. He was working as a night bellboy at a hotel. DeWayne went out the door without saying anything to us. The apartment was filled with fumes and a blue haze from the kerosene cookstove that was burning full blast heating a large pan of water. Mrs. Bond said that she paid thirty dollars a month for the apartment. She wouldn't have rented it, but she saw it at night and didn't see how dirty it was. She mentioned that she was back in her rent and that she did do a lot of work painting and cleaning it up. The living room walls were painted pink, and the ceiling was blue. The room was furnished with a threadbare, cheap blue chair and divan set, lamp tables and lamps at the end of the divan. Several pictures of black silhouette design and a Japanese feather bird picture hung upon the wall. Also there was a large framed wedding certificate with Holy Matrimony printed in large letters diagonally across smaller printing. A library table contained several pictures of the boys and of their relatives. A glass-topped coffee table that was very dusty showed the imprints of the ashtray when Mrs. Bond took it off the coffee table to catch her cigarette ashes. There was another stand with a lacy green fern and a large mahogany console radio that looked out of place due to its appearance. Except for the cheap worn living room linoleum and four red shag rugs and several other odd pieces of linoleum out in the kitchen the worn pine flooring was left uncovered. The kitchen contained a chrome set, two kerosene stoves, an old battered noisy refrigerator, washing machine, single cold-water tap at the small sink and a china closet. The adults' bedroom contained a cheap laminated light and dark wood, water-fall type bed with a chenille spread, dresser and chest set and several odd chairs.

Mrs. Bond is a frail and gaunt washed-out woman with a thin face. Her nose twitched nervously. She had thin lips that she frequently pulled down or screwed down at the corners from a nervous tic. She wore a net over her stringy greying blond hair. She nervously smoked several cigaretts and, although it was cool in the room, she perspired freely under the arms. Her blue loose-fitting cotton housedress hung from her shoulders like a sack. She wore cheap Indian moccasin houseslippers and seemed to be a little hard of hearing. Her speech and movements were rather slow, as if she was tired.

During the interview nothing was said about Mr. Fastelle, DeWayne's father, and I did not ask about him. He was the second husband of Mrs. Bond, who had children by all three of her husbands. There were at present three children at home—Dale, DeWayne, and a two-year-old girl.

Mrs. Bond said that DeWayne likes to earn money and that he has worked as a pin boy in bowling alleys. "He was always in things at school, too, when he was in elementary school. But he is not doing so much now in junior high school. He gets angry and cross when the teachers are mean to him, and I think that is what has happened at the junior high school. I find that if I talk nice to him I can get more out of him."

Talking about his health, she said, "He had creeping eczema when he was about two years old. I don't know if you know what that is like, but it is like somebody crying all the time. It seemed like tears were draining out around his ears and made large scabs. The doctor gave me some salve to clear it up and I gave him about four tubes and this seemed to clear it up. Just now he has a hurting in his stomach; I don't know what it is but he complains of pains in his stomach a good bit of the time."

"Does he have a good appetite?" Mrs. Bond, "Well, I don't have any trouble that way. He never stops to eat; he just comes into the house and fixes himself some bread or something. So does the other boy. Of an evening I always have supper fixed but they never seem to want to eat much. I work a lot of nights and then Mr. Bond heats something that I have left for them. I work at the State Tavern on Sixth Street.

"How do the two boys get along together?"

"Well, according to brothers I think they get along good. They do fight and argue but if someone outside tries to pick on one of them they are all into it."

"Mrs. Bond, do you have much trouble keeping track of DeWayne?"

"Well, he's too big now for me to pay much attention. Anyway, when I work evenings I don't have time to see to him, except to make him baby sit nights when my husband can't be here!"

"Are there any men that DeWayne likes and feels close to?"

"Yes, there's the man that runs recreation over at the Housing Project. I can't think of his name but he makes recreation to keep the children out of meanness. DeWayne used to go to Boy Scouts at the school but something happened and he dropped out. I never did know why, but I couldn't keep it up either with the money they needed for uniforms and things like that."

"What do you do in your spare time, Mrs. Bond?"

"Well, sometimes, not very often, I go to the show with my husband. But I don't generally have any place to go and most of my spare time I sleep."

Home Visit—Roy Cranston. This visit was made when Roy was just 16 and had dropped out of school. Roy had done poorly in school, had always had trouble with reading. His IQ was about 80. On sociometric tests when he' was 13 and 15 years old, he was seen by his age-mates as one of the most aggressive boys. His teachers saw him as about the most aggressive boy in the class.

The following anecdote illustrates the boy's hot temper. After he had dropped out of school, he was interviewed about his present job and his earlier school experience. He was asked about teachers he liked best and least, and he had the following to say about Mr. Albright, seventh grade teacher.

Albright—he was the one I liked the least. I still don't care much for him. What started it all over at Garfield, I was helping the principal with some tables in the gym. He sent a few of us down to do the job. They had a new floor on the gym. Anyway, I had trouble with Albright before, and he held a grudge. And I was always smarting off to him. Well, some kids were playing basket-ball on this new floor with shoes on. Albright came in there and yelled at me to get out of the gym. He blew his stack and I said, "You tell those other guys to get out and I'll get out." He grabbed me by the neck and arm and about broke my arm off, and I knocked him on his rump down three or four steps. I went up to the office and told the principal to call him off of me or I'd kill Albright. Albright started smarting off, and I got mad and threw some books at him. Later, he accused me of putting paint on his car at Halloween. It was two of his pets and the most sissified kids in the class that did it.

The report on the home visit is as follows:

The Cranston family lives in a small deteriorating brick house with apparently two rooms downstairs and possibly one or two rooms upstairs under a small gabled roof. The house is closely hemmed in by sub-standard dwellings on either side. Several large elm trees near the street shade the front yard, which is small and without grass. Roots from the elm trees have spread through the surface of the front yard causing the brick walks across the front of the house and leading to the house to buckle in places. There is no landscaping in the front yard. The brick walk leads past the east side of the house and one long cement step runs across two doors, one an entrance to the front room and the other to the kitchen. There is a screen at the kitchen door; the screen is rusty, and the door frame and door both had a dirty chipped grey paint. Roy was home alone when I called the first time; he was combing his slick black hair at the kitchen sink. The kitchen looked dark and dingy with a table piled with dirty dishes and cereal boxes. Roy did not bother to come to the door, he talked to me from the sink, apparently thinking I was a school representative trying to talk him into returning to school. He told me to return late in the day to see his mother. When I found her at home it was difficult to explain my purpose to her. She is a short plump woman, rather sloppy in dress and with black kinky hair parted on the side. She has big brown eyes and a round, rather friendly face. Her smile exposed large gaps between her upper front teeth. She wore a blue cotton housedress and black house slippers. She thought I was trying to urge Roy into returning to school. She said that she thought he should go too but that she wasn't going to force him. After I explained that I was not here for that purpose she could see no special reason for our spending the time on an interview, as long as the boy is no longer in school. She finally agreed for me to return on a Saturday morning and concluded by saying that if she was present we would talk and if she wasn't we would just forget it. Therefore I hardly expected her to be home when I called on Saturday. She did not take me into the house and suggested that it might be cooler back on a long picnic table in the rear yard. She led the way back to a shaded spot.

The rear yard was cluttered somewhat with old scraps of metal including an old lawn mower and parts of a car motor. There was an old-style Ford parked in the back yard. There was a fenced area with several mallard ducks caged up. Mrs. Cranston said that her husband uses them for decoys although they are not legal in hunting. There were some hoop fishing nets suspended over the fencing. She said that her husband has done quite a bit of commercial fishing on the side. She said that he works as a construction worker for the union; she means that the union gets him employment on construction jobs from time to time. She is employed at the Washington Laundry at the moment and Roy has been working with her at the laundry since about a week ago. Other members of the family are Fay, 18, who is employed as a waitress, Patricia, age 15, who will be a sophomore in High School, and James, 2. I re-explained the purpose of the Commission since she had a little trouble in understanding what we are doing. She commented that she had only gone to the eighth grade in school and that her husband had only finished the sixth grade.

I asked how Roy got along as an infant. She said, "He was just a little monkey. He was the smallest baby I had, he is fairly tall now. He was always quick about doing things, quick moving." "Was he a bottle baby or breast fed?" "He was a bottle baby." "Was he troubled with colic or any other illnesses as an infant?" "He had a little colic, I think all the kids did, but it wasn't too bad." "What were some of the difficulties that you had with Roy?" "Well it seemed he was so tiny and delicate. I don't remember that he was sick very much but we always thought that he might be. We were more concerned about him than we were with the others. We wondered if his heart was quite right and whether everything was going to be all right." "Did the doctor say that his heart wasn't good?" "No I don't remember the doctor ever saying that." "How did you get along during your pregnancy before Roy's birth?" "You see I had Roy and Patsy very close together, after them I had a fallen stomach and was bothered with nerves. I had an operation for that and was better then. The doctor said that I could not have any more babies, but then after Jamie was born I felt better than ever. When I used to take Jamie into the doctor he would ask me, "How is the little mistake?"

"Do you remember how Roy's older sister took to him when he was born?" "I just can't remember that." "Do you remember how Roy took to the younger ones when they were born?" "I can't remember that either. I know they all liked Jamie a lot and they all helped take care of him."

"What kind of day does Roy have at the present time? By that I mean just how does he get along with everybody at different times of the day, like breakfast and meal time and bed time?" "Well right now I don't even know where he is. I guess he is at some boy friend's house. He must have gone there last night, but he didn't let us know. He talked to me a few weeks ago about staying overnight with a boy on the farm and then working the next day to earn a little money. I told him that I didn't think he should and he said, "Why, I did that before," and that was the first I knew about it. He doesn't always tell me what he is doing. I suppose he was out at that farm last night or at one of his friends in town. When they get to be about 16 years old you just don't know where they are and I can understand it. I was married when I was 16 years old and my hubby is the kind that went on his own pretty young. He thinks it is all right for a boy to be that way. But Roy is a pretty good boy. He will scrub the floor or wash clothes and iron his own clothes. I always say he will make a pretty good woman for somebody. He doesn't mind too well and you have to coax him a lot to do things."

"Do you find that he loses his temper around the house pretty easy?" "Oh yes he is hotheaded and if he gets against us he is fighting mad." "Did this happen much when he was in school?" "Yes I think it did. Now he has helped out at Washington Laundry the past week. He came home the other night and said that someone was flipping an old towel at him and that he had a notion to tell him off. He is a boy who won't be run over. He gets to looking kind of droopy once in a while and I think it is because he is out so late. I notice that down at work. I didn't think he would stay with it and I asked him the other day, "Well, Roy, when are you going to quit this job? But he surprised me. He said, "Why should I quit, I'm just getting started." "What do you find works best for discipline with Roy when he does something wrong?" "Generally we just talk to him or give him a good booting. Most of the time just talking does best I think." "What sort of things do you have to discipline him for?" "I don't remember just off hand. Maybe he won't do something that you tell him to—like burning the rubbish. Then you have to give him a good talking to or a bat. It isn't anything awful bad though."

"What sort of things do you feel he is old enough to decide for himself?" "He decides quite a bit, I guess, but I like to have him tell me what he is going to do like when he is going to stay out at a friend's house. I think he should let us know that.

"How does Roy get along with other members of the family at present?" "He gets along well enough except when he gets one of these spells, and then he'd just as soon knock them down as not. Then other times he will be real quiet just a-stewing." "What do you mean by that?" "He sort of clams up and then he won't want to talk."

"I don't know about Roy in school. I just don't know why he didn't take to it. He was in St. Joseph's parochial school until about the fourth or fifth grade. Then he went to Garfield. They didn't seem to think they could do much for him at St. Joseph's. He couldn't get the reading and they weren't very anxious for him to go on there."

"Do Roy and his sister do much together or do they have their own interests?" "I think mostly they have their own interests."

"What sort of things does he do that you wish he wouldn't?" "Like at night time we think he ought to be in by 10:30 but he don't usually get in then. Of course, his father has the idea that at his age he should be pretty much on his own. Then I think he ought to let us know when he stays overnight. We should know a little more about him and what he is doing." "What sort of things is Roy rather successful at?" "He is pretty good at jobs like cleaning up yards. He has also helped deliver papers for two of his buddies, although he didn't have a paper route of his own." "What would you say gives you the most pleasure about Roy?" Here she giggled and said, "I don't know, I know I have laughed at him at times but I don't remember what for." "What gives you the most worry or concern about Roy?" "I don't really know that either. He talks about going into the Navy. You kind of hate to see them go into something like that, yet it might bring him out of these funny ways he has. It might end his flying off the handle. A boy has to learn to take it, and that is Roy's trouble. Then, he is kind of like me. I got in a rut staying here in the house and got so I didn't know what people were doing and what clothes people were wearing. You can get way down in the dumps. He is kind of like me and he needs to see more people and see how they are doing and acting. You can stay home and get to feeling sorry for yourself. I haven't been working very long at the Laundry and I still sort of feel that I belong at home, but then I see other people who have more children than I have and worry less about them. I suppose I shouldn't feel down like I do sometimes, and probably I'm not really needed at home."

"Has Mr. Cranston been able to help you much in raising the kids or have you had most of the responsibility?" "He thinks I'm the one who should tell the kids what to do because I'm here with them most of the time or at least had been until I started work. But I can't get them to do things very easy. When he is home he will tell them and flog them quicker than I will. They sort of wear me down." "Do you mean he is more quick-tempered than you are?" "No, he isn't quick-tempered but he will just boot them quicker to get them to move." She laughed and said, "He hasn't killed any of them yet. Then they sort of hold it against me. It is that old grind of telling them too many times to do something and they sort of blame me for having to tell them. I tell Roy and Patsy to do something so many times. When they won't do it, I'll tell my husband and then they had better do it."

"What does your hubby do in his spare time? "He hunts and fishes and goes to car races." While we were talking about him, Mr. Cranston backed another old model car into the yard from the alley. He is a husky guy of medium height with a large flushed face. He was neatly dressed wearing a summer cap, a tan sport shirt, blue wash pants and cloth shoes. He pushed the little two-year-old a bit in a swing near our bench and then sat down with us.

"Who are some of Roy's best pals?" Mr. Cranston answered, "Butch Francis, and I guess Jack Muller. Jack is his best friend, I guess, and he also pals with Ernie Lane." "What sort of things do the kids do together?" Mr.: "They swim and fish. They swim some at Indian Mounds and also up at Twin Oaks in the Bay." "Does Roy belong to any groups or clubs of any kind?" Mrs.: "No, he wasn't very handy at that sort of thing, and he has never attended church very much." Mr.: "He likes to bowl, and he used to set pins for a while." "What sort of things do you folks enjoy doing together?" Mrs.: "We go boat riding quite a bit."

"What do you think of the schools? Do you think there is anything the schools might have done to make Roy enjoy it a little more?" Mrs.: "He just didn't seem to care for school except arithmetic. He had trouble with reading when he was real young, and he never did learn to read very well, then he would get disgusted and lose interest. Somehow he missed something, where Patsy seemed to get it. Roy did better since he left St. Joseph's."

"Are you and Mrs. Cranston active in any organizations or church auxiliaries?" Mrs.: "I belong to the St. Joseph's Church, me and the kids belong but my husband doesn't. I don't belong to the auxiliary or anything like that. I guess I could but just never did." "What do you enjoy doing, Mrs. Cranston?" "Oh, I like to go to shows. I like to have parties for the kids. And I enjoy getting with other people a little bit."

"As a family group, do you do much with other families?" "Well, we like to go to people's houses and eat their cooking once in a while, as long as they leave the heavy drinking out. I don't go for that. I like to go to church, but I don't get there very regular. My husband doesn't go, but I get a lot out of the church. Religion has helped me, too, a lot. I really hated to take Roy out of the St. Joseph's School, but they said they couldn't help him out much. They said I should take him to Center School at that time. They said there was some special class up there for boys who had trouble in learning to read. I couldn't find it. I called out there but never did find it. Then one of my neighbors said she would arrange for him to go to Garfield School. And that is how he happened to go over there."

"In what ways do you feel that you have been rather successful with Roy, and in what way do you feel that you may have fallen down with Roy and you might do things differently if you could do them again." Mr. answered, "It would have been much better if Roy had started school over at Garfield instead of St. Joseph's. He should have been working on studies instead of all that catechism during those first years of school."

Mrs. Cranston kind of laughed and slapped him on the back. She said, "Well, they have a fine program of learning religion over there. It didn't seem to keep Patsy from getting her regular work but somehow Roy just didn't get it." Mr.: "Well, that's my belief and I got a right to it. I don't care what religion people have just so they don't try to convert me, and let me alone." Mrs.: "Somehow, Roy just didn't care about school; then I know they tried to push him over at St. Joseph's, and that just aggravated him. There for awhile, I was in the hospital, and I know he had a rough time then." Mr.: "Ya, I remember when you were in the hospital. They sent Patsy home one day with a note, that I should keep her home until she had her lessons prepared. I couldn't understand that. If they had sent that with Roy I could have. Not with her. I took that note and Patsy and went right over to school. I really got on them about that. After that, the teacher treated Patsy a lot better too."

We talked for a few minutes longer about Mr. Cranston's fishing side line, and then I departed leaving the two of them in the back yard.

Our ratings of the family relations of the two boys are given in Table 20. We gave DeWayne's home a score of 399 and Roy's home

TABLE 20. THE GLUECK DELINQUENCY PREDICTION SCALE APPLIED TO TWO BOYS

Family Quality	Score Value	DeWayne	Roy
1. Discipline of boy by father			
Overstrict or erratic	72		
Lax	60	X	
Firm but kindly	9		X
2. Supervision of boy by mother			
Unsuitable	83	X	
Fair	58		X
Suitable	10		
3. Affection of father for boy			
Hostile	84		
Indifferent	73	X	
Warm	34		X
4. Affection of mother for boy			
Hostile	87		
Indifferent	86	X	
Warm	43		X
5. Cohesiveness of family			
Unintegrated	97	X	
Some elements of cohesion	61		
Cohesive	21		X
Prediction Score		399	165

a score of 165.   According to Glueck's data, DeWayne had 89 chances
in 100 of becoming delinquent, and Roy had about 8 chances in 100.

DeWayne's first brush with the law came when he was 10 years old
and was brought before the police matron with some other boys for
putting their footprints in some freshly laid cement.   By the time he
was 16 he had an assortment of misbehaviors on the record, including
stealing and fighting and sexual offenses.

From the time he quit school at 16 until he was 17, DeWayne loafed
around town with cronies, getting unskilled jobs for a few weeks at a
time, and getting into various kinds of trouble.   Finally he enlisted
in the Navy.   He falls into category II of delinquency.

Roy, on the other hand, got a job as soon as he quit school at 16,
and has been working steadily ever since.   He married when he was
18, and has been leading a stable responsible life.   Roy had the advantage of a home which was cohesive, of warm affection from both
father and mother, and of a degree of firm but kindly discipline from
his father.   This probably gave him enough inner control to hold his
temper in check as he grew older.   When he dropped out of school
he was rid of the frustrations from that source, and he found legitimate
satisfaction in his work and his wife.   Roy will probably be a tough,
profane, lower-class man like his father.   He will probably break the
game laws by shooting ducks and taking fish illegally, but he will not
do the senseless, violent, aggressive things that we see in boys with
inadequate family experience.

Thus it appears that on the basis of a home interview that can
serve as a basis for rating on the Delinquency Prediction Scale, the
boys with high aggressive-maladjustment scores might be separated
into two groups.   One group is almost certain to contain mainly future
delinquents, while the other contains boys whose families are stable
and affectionate enough to save them from delinquency, even though
they show a great deal of unpleasant and aggressive behavior in
school and among their peers.

Although we did not secure home interviews for all of the boys with
high aggressive-maladjustment scores, we did secure them for a fair
number, together with interviews of others who were not especially
high in aggression but who dropped out of school.   The results of
these interviews are shown in Table 21.   The boys are listed in order
of their Delinquency Prediction Score.   This score appears to be useful in separating future delinquents from nondelinquents.   There was
only one boy with a low Delinquency Prediction Score who became
delinquent, and his was a low (category III) level of delinquency.

It should be noted that this is not a rigorous test of the Glueck De-

TABLE 21. DELINQUENCY AND FAMILY RELATIONS. DELINQUENCY PREDICTION SCORES, BASED ON HOME VISITS, IN RELATION TO RECORD OF ACTUAL DELINQUENCY

| | Aggressive | Family Relations Category | | | | | | |
Social Class of Boy	Malad-justment T-Score	Discipline by Father	Supervision by Mother	Affec'n fr. Father	Affec'n fr. Moth.	Cohesiveness of Family	Prediction Score	Actual Level of Delinquency
D	76	60	83	73	86	97	399	II
D	75	60	83	73	86	97	399	II
C	67	60	83	73.	86	61	375	I
D	73	72	83	73	43	97	368	I
D	74	72	58	73	43	61	307	II
B	70	60	58	73	43	61	295	II
D	75	60	10	73	86	61	290	III
D	—	9	58	73	86	61	287	II
C	70	9	58	73	86	61	287	III
D	69	60	58	73	43	21	255	III
D	70	60	10	73	43	61	247	III
C	76	9	10	73	86	61	239	I
D	66	72	10	34	43	61	220	No
C	63	60	10	73	43	21	207	No
C	72	60	10	34	43	21	168	No
C	60	9	58	34	43	21	165	No
B	65	9	10	34	43	21	117	III
D	51	9	10	34	43	21	117	No
B	47	9	10	34	43	21	117	No
C	38	9	10	34	43	21	117	No
C	60	9	10	34	43	21	117	No
B	66	9	10	34	43	21	117	No

Note: The score for Aggressive Maladjustment is a *T*-score, with the mean at 50. The 90th percentile is about 63 on this scale, and the 95th percentile is 67.

Prediction Score	Chances of Becoming Delinquent
less than 200	8 in 100
200–249	37 in 100
250–299	64 in 100
300 and over	89 in 100

linquency Prediction Scale, for two reasons. One reason is that the interviews were made when the boys were aged 14 to 17, whereas for predictive purposes they should have come when the boys were younger than 12. Nevertheless, the interview was aimed at finding out about the family relations of the boy when he was younger, and the ratings were made as far as possible on this basis. The other reason is that the boys whose parents were interviewed were not a representative sample of the group. They were interviewed either because the boy was aggressive or because the boy had dropped out of school. Therefore Table 21 can only be said to give an indication that the Glueck Prediction Scale is useful when used to supplement data on social maladjustment and school failure.

Conclusions

Delinquency among boys in River City takes the form of theft, drunkenness, destruction of property, fighting, sexual offenses, and traffic violations. There is little or no gang fighting, and no drug addiction. Among girls there is much less delinquency of the kind that brings contact with the police. Only one-seventh as many girls as boys had a delinquency record of any consequence.

Almost without exception, the delinquents were failures in school and dropped out at about the age of 16. Their failure in school was not only academic; but also it was social, in the sense that they did not get along well with their peers in school, and they disliked the social life of the school, feeling that they were objects of prejudice and discrimination.

There is evidence that a stable, affectionate family can keep a boy out of delinquency even though he is a failure in school, grows up in a lower-class culture, and has a record and reputation of aggressive maladjustment in school.

Thus delinquency appears to be a part of a process of failure to grow up successfully. This failure shows itself by the age of 10 or 11 in the form of failure in school and in some form of aggressive maladjustment. When a boy of this type reaches his teens he has increasing trouble in finding legitimate forms of success. He drops out of school and has trouble finding and holding a job. Unless his family has given him some inner moral control and emotional security, he has a strong likelihood of becoming delinquent.

The most effective preventive measures against juvenile delinquency seem to be (1) finding ways of improving the family life of socially and economically underprivileged boys and girls and (2) finding ways of making school a more successful and satisfying part of their lives, or (3) creating an alternative pathway to adulthood for boys through work experience and helping them to follow this pathway. Chapter 10 describes such a work experience program.

7

≋

YOUTH AND THE CHURCH

ONE OF THE PRINCIPAL INSTITUTIONS for social and personal development of youth in American society is the church. It is expected to have a positive effect over and above that of the family and that of the school.

River City is generally thought to be well-churched. There are 32 Protestant congregations, 8 Roman Catholic, one Jewish, and one Bahai. Among the Protestant groups are included the Salvation Army and several fundamentalist sects which are strongest among the working class, as well as the high-status Protestant Episcopal Church and the liberal humanist Unitarian Church. On a Sunday the Catholic churches are busy with a series of masses from early morning till noon, and several of the Protestant churches have two morning services in order to accommodate all their worshippers.

On weekdays most of the churches have a calender of activities that provide something for all ages. Boy Scout activities are organized frequently within the churches. The Catholic Youth Organization has an active weekday recreation program.

The Study of Relationship to Church

The study of relationship to the church was made in 1958, when most of the boys and girls were 17 or 18 years old. Each of 42 clergymen or responsible leaders of religious groups was given a list of

89

430 names of boys and girls in the study group. (From the total list of 487, the names were removed of those who had moved out of the community at least two years before the church study was made, leaving 430 who were in the community at the time, or had been in the community recently.) Forty-one clergymen responded, and information on the remaining congregation was secured from laymen in that church.

The clergymen were asked to indicate all youths who were known to them as participants in their church, to indicate the membership status of the youth and his family, to rate the frequency of attendance, and to give their judgment of the significance of religious belief, affiliation, and participation to the individual. They were also asked to indicate those boys and girls who showed outstanding leadership in church-related activities.

The ratings of significance of the church to the individual were placed in two categories:

The church has some importance in the life of this person.
This person is known to me as an occasional participant in the church, but does not show by his attendance or participation that the church has any importance to him.

This left a group of boys and girls who were unknown as participants to any clergyman, and provided three categories of relation to the church, which are used in the tables of this chapter. Of the group 43 per cent were reported by the clergy as church members.

Social Class and Church Relationship

Table 22 shows how social class and sex are related to church activity and interest. Of the total group, 61 per cent were known to a clergyman, and 35 per cent were judged by the clergy to find some importance in the church for themselves.* Girls were more active in

* It is interesting to compare these data with those on church participation of adults. In a study of a Midwestern county made at about the same time as this study was made, it was found that 30 to 40 per cent attended church regularly (41 or more times a year); another 30 to 40 per cent attended intermittently, while the remainder have almost no contact with a church. This is rather similar to the pattern of youth participation in River City. See Victor Obenhaus, W. Widdick Schroeder, and Charles D. England, "Church Participation Related to Social Class and Type of Center." Rural Sociology. XXIII (September 1958), 298–308.

the church and better known to the clergy than were boys. There is a marked relation between church participation and social class, with higher-status youth much more active in church. The only exception to this rule is the high proportion of A Class boys (40 per cent) who were unknown to a clergyman. However, this was actually a small

TABLE 22. CHURCH RELATIONSHIP AND SOCIAL CLASS

Church Relation Category	Class A		Class B		Class C		Class D		Total Group	
	M	F	M	F	M	F	M	F	M	F
Church is important	30	63	43	55	31	39	14	16	30	40
Known to church, but church is not important	30	32	30	29	19	31	14	33	21	31
Unknown to clergy	40	5	27	16	50	30	72	51	49	29
Number	20	19	56	56	86	84	58	51	220	210

Note: The numbers in the table are percentages of the various social-class groups, Reprinted with permission from Robert J. Havighurst and Bernice L. Neugarten. *Society and Education,* 2nd Edition. Boston: Allyn and Bacon, Inc. 1962. Table 7.2.

number (8 boys) and may have been an accidental feature of this particular group.

Intelligence, Progress through School, and Church Relationship

Those with higher intelligence were more likely to be interested in church than were those with lower intelligence, as is seen in Table 23, which compares the top 25 per cent in intelligence with the total group. It is interesting in this connection that a sex difference is not evident in this table. The more intelligent boys are as likely to be interested in church as are the more intelligent girls.

There is also a relationship between progress through school and church activity, with those who get the most education being more interested in the church. This is shown in Table 24. Here the effects of intelligence and of social class and educational motivation are combined.

Compared with boys and girls of equal social class and IQ, as seen in Chapter 5, dropouts are unknown to clergymen in 67 per cent of the cases, whereas their controls are unknown in only 22 per cent of the cases.   Less than 20 per cent of the dropouts were church members and only one was rated a leader in his church, compared to over 50 per cent members and 10 per cent leaders in the control group.

TABLE 23. CHURCH RELATIONSHIP AND INTELLIGENCE (PER CENT OF YOUTH IN THE TOP 25 PER CENT OF IQ WHO APPEAR IN THE VARIOUS CHURCH RELATIONSHIP CATEGORIES)

Church Relation Category	Top 25 Per cent of IQ		Total Group	
	M	F	M	F
Church is important	64	62	30	40
Known to church but church is unimportant	21	22	21	31
Unknown to clergy	15	16	49	29
Number	48	58	220	210

Note: The numbers in the table are percentages of the groups indicated.

TABLE 24. CHURCH RELATIONSHIP AND AMOUNT OF EDUCATION

Church Relation Category	Dropout				Hi. Sch. Graduate	College Entrant	Total Group
	Grades 7, 8, 9	Grade 10	Grade 11	Grade 12			
Church is important	0	12	18	29	45	62	35
Known to church, but church is not important	14	27	27	33	31	24	26
Unknown to clergy	86	61	55	38	24	14	39
Number	51	33	40	24	164	93	430

Note: Numbers in the Table are percentages of the groups according to highest educational level.

Among those with relatively low ability (IQ between 75 and 90) there are some who do fairly well in school and others who do very poorly.   The difference between them seems to lie largely in their educational motivation and their social adjustment.   A comparison was made between a group of 62 boys and girls of this IQ range who

were failing in the eighth grade and 22 of the same IQ who were doing satisfactory school work, somewhat above the level that would be
expected from their measured intelligence. Among the failing group,
the percentages in the three church categories (important, unimportant, unknown to clergy) were 20, 31, and 49 respectively. Among
the academically successful group the percentages were 59, 5, and 36
respectively.

Here, too, the youth with greater academic success have much more
interest in the church than do those who are failing.

Social and Personal Adjustment and Church Relationship

The relations between church activity and social and personal adjustment can be explored in several ways. One measure of personal
adjustment was the California Psychological Inventory, given to the
study group when they were in the tenth grade of high school, and
after some had dropped out of school. Scores on the Inventory were
computed in the form of T-scores, with an average for the total group
of 50 and a standard deviation of 10. Those who were unknown to
any clergymen had an average score of 47.0, which is substantially below the average of the total group. Those for whom church was

TABLE 25. CHURCH RELATIONSHIP AND SOCIAL AD-
JUSTMENT

Church Relation Category	Total Group	Social Leader-ship	Aggres-sion	With-drawal	Delin-quency Males only
Church is important	35	71	33	35	14
Known to church, but church is not important	26	12	8	11	13
Unknown to clergy	39	17	59	54	73
Number		84	86	83	78

Note: Categories I, II and III for delinquency are included. Category IV
(low delinquency level) is excluded. This table is based on a study of two
age-groups, separated by two years in age, one of which was the study group
around which this book is organized. The findings are similar for the two
age-groups, and gain greater stability when the two groups are combined.
The numbers in the table are percentages of the groups described at the top
of each column.

judged to be unimportant had an average score of 47.6, and those for whom church was judged to be important had an average score of 51.4. The group who were identified as leaders in church activities had an average score of 53.7. Thus those who were interested and active in church had significantly higher adjustment scores than did those who were uninterested or unknown to the church.

Other ways of looking at the relation of adjustment to church activity show the same results. They are summarized in Table 25. Measures of adjustment are the combined sociometric test scores and teacher ratings for social leadership, aggression, and withdrawal. The 10 per cent scoring highest on these measures are reported in Table 25, together with the boys who were in categories I, II, and III of delinquency, as defined in Chapter 6. Church was regarded as important, by the clergy, for 71 per cent of those high in social leadership, and for 14 per cent of the delinquent boys. More than half of those who were severely maladjusted were unknown to any clergyman.

Church Leaders and School Leaders among Youth

The clergymen were asked to indicate the boys and girls who showed a high level of leadership in church activities. They named 99 persons from two age groups (the Study Group and the group two years younger). For these two age groups there were data on social leadership from sociometric tests and teacher ratings made in grades 4 through 9. The 90 with highest scores have been called "school leaders." Thus there were about 10 per cent of the total group identified as leaders in church activities on the one hand, and 10 per cent identified as leaders in the school environment on the other hand.

There was an overlap of 30 cases, whose names appeared on both leadership lists. Although this was far more than could have occurred by chance, it indicates, nevertheless, that the church finds two-thirds of its youthful leaders from a group who do not appear as leaders in school, and vice versa. In both groups of leaders, the social-class distribution was almost exactly the same, the percentages being 20, 39, 34, and 7 in social classes A, B, C, and D respectively.

Conclusions

The results of the study of interest and participation in the church by adolescents of River City are internally consistent. Boys and girls from families of higher status are far more likely to be seen by the clergy as interested in and active in the church. Boys and girls of greater intelligence, and those who are more successful in school, are also more likely to be active in church. Finally, boys and girls who are better adjusted personally and socially are more likely to be interested in church than are those who are maladjusted.

The interpretation of these results is not clear. One person may say that this proves that the church is doing a good job for those with whom it comes into contact, but that there are many others whom the church does not help who need help and would profit from more attention by the church. Another person may say that these findings indicate that the church mainly serves those who need it least, those who are higher in social status and who are already getting along well in school and community.

There is certainly no evidence here of the redeeming power of the church in River City. On the other hand, a more intensive study would certainly show that a number of boys and girls (although admittedly a small number) have been greatly helped by the church to overcome handicaps of personal inferiority and social background when home and school were inadequate for them. The fact that two-thirds of the church youth leaders are not school leaders indicates that the church supplies something important for this subgroup.

There might be general agreement on two conclusions: first, that the church cooperates with school and home to help the most successful boys and girls to grow up well; and second, that there is a very large group of boys and girls who are unsuccessful or at the most indifferently successful, with whom the church has no contact at all.

THE YOUNG ADULT

8

~~~~~

WHO GOES TO COLLEGE?

FOR YOUNG PEOPLE who succeed in graduating from high school, the road to adulthood branches at this point, one branch leading directly to full-time employment, one to marriage and home-making, and one to college. These branches represent choices among socially acceptable alternatives, although college has become increasingly popular since the second World War, and there is a growing social expectation that boys and girls in the abler half of the group should go to college.

Slightly under 30 per cent of the River City study group entered college or some other post-secondary institution the first year after graduation from high school. Post-secondary institutions not of college grade were hospital schools of nursing and a local business college, which attracted girls mainly. More boys than girls went on to college. Table 26 shows how intellectual ability and social status are related to college-going in this cohort.

These figures compare with 40 per cent of boys and 27 per cent of girls entering college for the first time in 1958 in the United States, when the numbers are compared with the population aged 18. These percentages include a good many who entered college after delay of a year or more subsequent to high school graduation, mainly boys who had been in the armed services. Consequently the River City figures underestimate the proportions of this cohort who will eventually enter college. Probably the proportion of this cohort who enter college will be slightly smaller than the national proportion.

TABLE 26. SOCIAL CLASS AND INTELLIGENCE IN RELATION TO POST HIGH SCHOOL EDUCATION (NUMBERS OF BOYS AND GIRLS)

Quartile for IQ	Highest Level	Male					Female				
		A	B	C	D	Total	A	B	C	D	Total
IV High	Post hi. schl	0	0	0	0	0	1	2	3	0	6
	Col. dropout	1	2	0	0	3	0	0	1	0	1
	College	6	10	7	1	24	11	10	8	0	29
III	Post hi. schl	0	0	0	0	0	0	1	3	0	4
	Col. dropout	1	4	2	0	7	0	0	1	0	1
	College	6	6	3	0	15	3	7	3	0	13
II	Post hi. schl	0	0	1	0	1	0	1	0	1	2
	Col. dropout	1	0	2	0	3	0	0	0	0	0
	College	0	3	0	0	3	0	1	0	0	1

I	Post hi. schl	0	0	0	0	1	0	1	0	2
	Col. dropout	0	1	0	2	1	0	0	0	1
	College	0	1	0	1	1	0	0	0	1
Total	Post hi. schl	0	0	1	1	2	4	7	1	14
	Col. dropout	3	7	4	15	1	0	2	0	3
	College	12	20	10	43	15	18	11	0	44
	Grand total	15	27	15	59	18	22	20	1	61

Note: Post high school means work in a nordegree course, generally business or nursing.
College dropout means did not complete the first year of college successfully.
College means completed the first year of college successfully, and can continue.

As can be seen in Table 26, over half of the college entrants came from the top quartile of intellectual ability, while about one-tenth came from the bottom half of intellectual ability. As for social status, Class B, the lower-middle, provides more college students than do Classes A or C, whereas Class D, the lower-lower class, sends no girls to college and almost no boys. Classes A and C send almost equal numbers to college, but Class A sends relatively 75 per cent of its youth to college whereas the much larger Class C (the upper-working class) sends about 20 per cent of its youth beyond high school (cf. Table V-1, Appendix).

These facts about the social-class origins of college students point to a social revolution that has occurred in the colleges since 1930. At that time the upper-middle class dominated the colleges. Now it provides less than a third of college students.

By the end of the first year of college attendance, one fourth of the boys who had entered dropped out, whereas only 6 per cent of the girls dropped out. This is not a good estimate of the eventual number of college dropouts, since many college students fail to return for the second or third year of college, and many girls, especially, drop out after two years of college. What Table 26 does indicate is that River City boys have more scholastic difficulties during the first year of college than girls do, a fact which is generally true of boys compared with girls throughout the country.

The existence of two small church-related liberal arts colleges, one in River City and one within commuting distance, makes it relatively easy for young people with limited financial resources to go to college while living at home. Actually, 27 of 105 college entrants attended these two colleges. There was a tendency for the lower-status youth to go to the local colleges. Eleven of 16 Class C and D boys and 6 of 13 Class C and D girls entered these colleges. In contrast, only 1 of 15 class A boys and 1 of 16 Class A girls entered the local Colleges.* The lower-status boys were more likely to enter the local colleges than were the lower-status girls.

Intelligence and Personal Adjustment in Relation to College Attendance

The fact that youth of above-average intellectual ability are much more likely than those with below-average ability to enter college is

---

* The chi-square test of the null hypothesis gives a p-value of .01 for boys, and .02 for girls.

shown clearly in Table 27, which reports the facts about college entrance for boys and girls in relation to their intelligence quotients.

With respect to personal-social adjustment, there is a strong tendency for those who are better adjusted to go to college. This is seen in Table 15 (Chapter 5), where those who have higher scores for adjustment are more likely than any other group to enter college. These adjustment data come from grades 6 and 7, and very similar results arise from a comparison of the California Psychological Inventory scores, taken in the tenth grade, with the college-entrance data.

TABLE 27. INTELLIGENCE IN RELATION TO COLLEGE ENTRANCE (PERCENTAGES SEPARATELY, BY SEX)

	Male		Female	
Quartile, for IQ	Entered College	Did not enter Col.	Entered College	Did not enter Col.
IV (high)	15	10	12	13
III	10	15	6	19
II	3	22	1	24
I	1	24	1	24
Number	58	155	47	172

Note: These data report on entrance to college in September after high school graduation in June. This underestimates the final result, since a number of youth, especially boys, will enter college later.

However, there are some important exceptions to the rule that good personal adjustment in the elementary school is predictive of college attendance. A few maladjusted elementary school children succeeded in entering college despite this handicap. This was true of 3 children among the 92 most severely maladjusted as described in Chapter 3. These three children had some advantages that were not typical of the maladjusted group as a whole. All three came from middle-class families, and religion was judged to be an important influence in their lives. None of the families was broken by divorce or separation, and all three children had been successful in school. All were in the top quarter in IQ and also in the top quarter of their high school class by school marks. Thus, though they were seen by teachers and peers as maladjusted in the sixth and seventh grades, these few boys and girls had great advantages which substantially offset their maladjustment.

MOTIVATION FOR COLLEGE

Assuming that all students in the upper quartile of intelligence have ample ability to make good use of college education, we see by Table 5-1 (Appendix) that about half of these girls and three-fifths of these boys entered college. This means that there was a "loss" to the colleges of half of the top quarter of girls and a third of the top quarter of boys. Although a few of them, mainly boys, will enter college later, there will remain a considerable number of able girls and boys who do not take advantage of college education.

Most of the able boys and girls who did not go to college came from Classes B, C, and D, as can be seen in Table 5-1. Their reasons for not going on to college are partly economic and partly motivational. The purely economic reason of lack of money has been shown in several studies to be less important than lack of motivation in preventing able young people from going to college. That motivation is more important than money in River City was clearly shown in interviews with the ablest quarter of the cohort. Those who did not go to college generally lacked a strong drive. If they had wanted to go to college, most of them could have borrowed or earned the money, although a few would have been prevented from going to college by sheer poverty or by responsibility for support of their families.

The motivation factor has been studied in some detail in this group of boys and girls and is presented for consideration.

Motivation, or desire for education, as we have seen in Chapter 4, arises from the following factors.

1. Need for achievement.
2. Identification with persons who have gone to college.
3. Social pressures.
4. Enjoyment of study.

The utmost motivation for college is found in a person who has a strong basic drive for achievement which he believes he can realize through college education; whose closest relatives and friends want him to go to college; and who enjoys study.

Among able people, those with high educational motivation make the most out of their education. In fact, differences in intellectual ability among those in the top quarter are likely to be less important in determining what kind of success a person makes in college and in later life than are differences in motivation, or in drive and purposes.

In studying the relations between motivation and college experience of River City youth we discovered that there were great differences between boys and girls in this respect. In fact, the general conclusions we have been able to draw about boys do not apply to girls. Therefore we discuss the sexes separately.

Motivation of Boys for College

While the members of this particular River City cohort were in the tenth grade, Dr. Eugene Stivers made a study of the motivation for college of the boys and girls in the top quarter of intellectual ability. He interviewed them about their plans for education and for work and classified them as "motivated for college" and "not motivated for college." The group that he studied numbered 63 girls and 46 boys. He classified 38 girls and 32 boys as "well-motivated for college," and 25 girls and 14 boys as "not motivated for college." His classification of boys gave successful predictions, since 27 of the 32 "motivated" boys went to college immediately after graduating from high school, and 12 of the 14 "not-motivated" boys did not go to college.

Need for Achievement. As a measure of the basic need for achievement Stivers used the test developed by McClelland, which has been described in Chapter 4. The score on this test is called n-Achievement. Stivers found that the boys who were well-motivated for college had a higher n-Achievement than those who were not motivated for college.

Identification and Social Pressures. In an interview, a student was asked what people and what agencies set college as a desirable goal for him—family, school teachers, age-mates, community leaders, books, etc. The interview was scored on the basis of the number of these influences that were favorable toward going to college, how intensively and how frequently they operated on the students and how close he felt to the people who advised him. Stivers found that those who were well-motivated for college had a significantly greater set of social pressures that had set college as a goal for them. That is, their parents, teachers, friends and others tended to encourage them strongly to go to college.

Enjoyment of Study. Stivers did not collect data systematically on the difference between the two groups of boys in enjoyment of study, although his interviews suggested that the college-motivated boys did indeed enjoy study more than did the nonmotivated boys. Furthermore, the comparison of achievers and non-achievers in high school in Chapter 4 showed that among the boys the high achievers had more academic interests and hobbies than did the low achievers. Since the high achievers were more likely to be well-motivated for college, this finding confirms the theory.

Personality. Stivers also used the California Psychological Inventory with his group, and found that the boys who were well-motivated for college scored higher on this Inventory than those who were not.

Educational Motivation of Boys Who Went to College. The study of motivation of able tenth grade boys for college was supplemented by

TABLE 28. COMPARISON OF BOYS WHO WENT TO COL-
LEGE WITH BOYS WHO DID NOT GO (UPPER QUARTER OF
INTELLECTUAL ABILITY)

		Went to College	Did not Go to College	
High achievers in high school		22	5	
Low achievers in high school		12	14	$p = .01$
Quartile rank in high school				
class: school marks	IV High	19	2	
	III	8	7	
	II	4	5	$p = .02$
	I	1	4	
	Unknown	2	1	
Social class	A	9	1	
	B	15	6	$p = .05$
	C	9	8	
	D	1	4	
Mean T-score on California				
Psychological Inventory		54.2	50.6	$p = .01$
n-Achievement	Grade 10	8.83	6.30	$p = .1$
	Grade 12	3.75	2.13	$p = .05$

a study of the same boys after they had graduated from high school. Therefore it was possible to compare boys who had gone to college with those who had not, and to compare college dropouts with those who completed the first year of college successfully. The data for this comparison are given in Table 28.

The boys who went to college were definitely superior in their school marks to those who did not go, and also in their school grades when these were seen in relation to their intellectual ability. That is, the able boys who did good school work relative to their ability were more likely to go to college than were the able boys who did average or poor school work.

There was a strong tendency for able boys of higher social status to go to college (9 out of 10 Class A boys), but boys of C and D status were much less likely to go to college.

The need for achievement of the boys who went to college was reliably greater than the need for achievement of those who did not go.

The personal-adjustment score (from the California Psychological Inventory) of the college-going boys was higher than that of those who did not go, although those who did not go to college had average scores on this instrument, compared with the total cohort of boys.

THE COLLEGE DROPOUTS. By the end of the first year after high school graduation, 15 of 58 college-entering boys had dropped

TABLE 29. COMPARISON OF SUCCESSFUL COLLEGE STUDENTS WITH COLLEGE DROPOUTS

	Successful in First Year	Dropped out in First Year
Intelligence	58.1	50.1
Social leadership	58.5	53.6
Number	85	17

Note: These are T-scores, with a mean of 50 and a standard deviation of 10 for the total study group.

out because of low grades or for other reasons. About half of these dropouts were below average in high school grades and probably found college work too difficult for them. Nevertheless, an equal number of below-average high school students were successful in their first year of college. There was a tendency for the college dropouts to fall below the college stayins in both intelligence and social adjustment as measured by the social-leadership score. This is shown in Table 29. We shall have occasion to see repeatedly that intelligence and social leadership reinforce each other to make for successful growth. In Table 29 those successful in college were almost a standard deviation higher than the dropouts in IQ and at least half a standard deviation higher in social-leadership score.

Who Did Not Go to College. Among the boys of upper quarter intellectual ability, it is interesting to find out about the characteristics of those who did not go to college. As Table 28 shows, there were 19 of these boys, compared with 34 who did go to college. This group of able noncollege boys tended to come from working-class homes, to have below-average or only average high school grades, to have lower need for achievement than did the college-going boys, and to have somewhat lower personality adjustment scores than able college-going boys. Thus, nonattendance in college is related statistically with a group of disadvantages—lower social status, lower school achievement, lower achievement drive, and lower personality adjustment score—as compared with college attendance among boys in the upper quarter of intellectual ability.

Some Typical Cases. Some of these differences between boys of superior ability who attend or who do not attend college can be illustrated by the following cases:

Paul. A lower-lower class boy with an extremely high n-Achievement score, Paul said: "My father and mother never went to college. I thought I'd like to go and do better in life than they did." As a child, Paul was placed in a boys' boarding school sponsored by a Protestant denomination. The superintendent and the teachers there were demanding but warm. When Paul went to the city high school, at first he did not do so well as he had in the boarding school. "English was about my worst subject. The teacher helped me though, and I improved a lot. I consider her an important person in my life." For a time Paul considered farming as an occupation, but a careers unit in civics class dissuaded him, and he turned to engineering and mathematics, which he enjoyed.

Neither of his divorced parents had ever suggested college to Paul, but two of his closest friends had college plans and the superintendent of the boys' home urged him to go. "He told me to go to college. He said I did good in school, and I ought to go."

Ralph. Ralph, an upper-lower class boy with a high n-Achievement score, planned to "attend the University and study to be a musician and a music teacher." In elementary school he had little competition and did well with scarcely any effort. His divorced mother had high hopes for him; both she and his older brother were proud of Ralph's success. In high school, apart from some difficulty in geometry, he continued to do well, especially in music. His mother and brother occasionally suggested college to him, and several of his best friends planned to go, but his greatest sources of encouragement were his music teachers and his own accomplishments in music.

"I once wanted to be a farmer. Father was one, and also a couple of uncles. But when we moved into town my grandfather, a musician, prophesied that I'd be one too. My mother also plays and sings a lot. I didn't get interested, though, until the seventh grade when I started my private music lessons. My present teacher, especially, has had a tremendous effect on me. With him, I built up my interest in music, and it's never dropped down. He has talked to me many times about going into music, and he told me that I'd have to choose between professional music and teaching. He built me up, maybe too much. After all, I'm no child prodigy; neither am I an idiot. To sum it up, my teachers have influenced me to become as good as they are. Dick (his best friend, who is also a good student and a musician) is an influence because whatever is good for him is good for me. And my ability to play and strive to perfect music and my understanding of music is an influence on me."

Tom. On the other hand, Tom, an upper-middle class boy with a below-average n-Achievement score, plans "to help Dad on the farm for a while, probably, then get a job in town. I'm not sure what kind. Then I'll try for something better and advance as much as I can." Tom's elementary-school years were spent in a rural school, where he did good work. In high school he did fairly well, though his teachers thought that he should do better. "I usually don't do as well in English as in other subjects," he said. His mother used to talk about college but has not mentioned the subject for several years. No other adult ever suggested that he attend college, and none of his close friends was going.

"We've lived on a farm since I was five, so I got kind of interested in farming. And Barry (Tom's best friend) belonged to the Future Farmers last year and told me about it, so I got interested in it. But when I first came to high school I took industrial arts, and down in electric shop I kind of got interested in that. So I joined the 4-H Club and went to electricity training school. My Dad thinks that I should get a job in town after high school; I don't know exactly what kind. Mother thinks so too; maybe some kind of carpentry work, because my father does a lot of that."

Alex. Alex, a lower-middle class boy with a very low n-Achievement score said: "I haven't really got an idea of what I'd like to do, but probably something that has to do with math. I don't know. If I decided to be a doctor or a lawyer, I could be a success, but I don't believe I want to go into it. I don't like stuff like that. I wouldn't want to be a lawyer or a doctor."

In elementary school his grades, especially in mathematics, were fairly good, and several teachers encouraged him to continue in this field. At the time of the study, however, his marks were dropping, though occasionally he received good grades in his favorite subject. Both his teachers and his parents thought he ought to do better, and Alex himself said: "I haven't lived up to my standards, either. I think I play around quite a bit in class." None of his close friends planned to attend college, and no adult except his father ever encouraged him to go. "He'd like for me to go to college and be a lawyer or doctor, but he doesn't talk about it too much."

Conclusions for Boys

For boys in our society there is an interrelated set of circumstances and forces that tends to send some to college while the absence of these things keep others out of college. These are: intellectual ability; socioeconomic status; examples set by parents and other "significant persons"; expectations of family, age-mates, and community; favorable personal adjustment; drive for achievement; and pleasure in study and doing things of an academic nature.

If it is desired to increase the proportion of boys going to college, there are two principal target groups to aim at. One is the lower-middle class group and the other is the upper-working class group. The boys with above-average intellectual ability in these two social classes make up 33 per cent of the total group of boys, but more than half of these boys, 18 per cent of the total group, do not go beyond high school.

If the school and community want to get more boys from this group into college, they should develop a program which would accomplish the following things:

1. Through an expanded counselling program in the junior and senior high school, identify the able boys not well-motivated for college and inform them and their parents of the possibility of college, and the advantages that might come from it. Also, inform the teachers about this group of boys who are good college material but not likely to go to college unless influenced by the school.

2. Through the skillful use of honor awards, assembly programs, clubs and other extracurricular activities, and through collaboration with service clubs and other community organizations, increase the social desirability and the social prestige of going to college.

3. Through the academic program of the school, and through selecting and training teachers, make school work more interesting and more rewarding to these boys. This is the crucial thing, but the least tangible of the three that have been mentioned. Some school programs are more interesting and more challenging to able boys and girls than others—that is a clear fact. Some teachers make their subjects so interesting that they win students and encourage them to continue a life of study. River City High School had two or three such teachers, who were well known to the colleges in the Middle West for having sent boys and girls to college with excellent grounding and great interest in their particular subjects.

Motivation of Girls for College

The educational motivation of girls is not only different from that of boys, but suffers a reversal at the close of high school which complicates the educational history of a cohort of girls, as we shall see. It is well known that girls do better than boys in school work throughout elementary and secondary school. They also do better in group intelligence tests up to the age of about 15, when boys begin to overtake them. In River City, among the top quartile in intelligence there were 42 boys and 68 girls in the cohort under study, the intelligence tests having been given mainly in the sixth grade.

These facts are generally explained on the ground that girls are more conforming to adult authority than boys are, and therefore do better in the adult-imposed tasks of the school. Expressed in terms of educational motivation, it is common to say that girls have higher motivation than boys for education through the secondary school, at least. Consequently girls get better school marks than boys, and more girls than boys graduate from high school.

If our society were dominated by women the obvious superiority of girls over boys in school work and in most measures of intellectual ability might be explained as due to innate superiority of the female over the male. However, the American society with its masculine domination prefers to explain the fact as due to greater educational motivation of girls, on the assumption that the sexes are equal in basic intellectual ability. There is some evidence for this assumption in that boys catch up with girls in intelligence tests during their teens, and men are not inferior to women in this respect.

At the end of the secondary school there is a sharp shift in the balance of educational motivation between the sexes. Whereas more girls than boys graduate from high school, more boys than girls enter college. On a nation-wide basis, 40 per cent of boys and 27 per cent of girls entered college in 1958 when the numbers of college entrants were compared with the numbers of 18-year-olds. More girls than boys enter post-secondary school institutions that do not grant a college degree, such as certain hospital schools of nursing, business colleges, or secretarial schools.

The major reason for this break in the educational pattern is that achievement and success in life are defined differently for boys and girls. Achievement and occupational success and progress up the educational ladder tend to be all part of the same pattern for boys in American society. For most girls, achievement and success in life are identified with successful marriage and motherhood first, and only in a subordinate way with a career. No doubt the career pattern has become much more widely recognized and accepted for American women in recent decades. Many women now successfully combine an occupational career with marriage and a family. However, most girls with substantial intellectual ability and achievement drive experience an inner conflict over the division of their time and energy between career and family life—in sharp contrast to most men, who find little conflict between their occupational roles and the roles of husband and father.

The Motivation for College of Able Girls

In Stivers' study he found that among girls in the top quarter of ability, those who were well motivated for college actually had less drive for achievement than those who were not motivated for college. However, those who were bound for college had more social pressure from family, friends and school to go to college than those not motivated for college—as was the case with boys. There was also a tendency of the girls motivated for college to have higher scores on certain sections of the California Psychological Inventory, dealing with intellectual efficiency and with responsibility.

It seems clear that a drive for achievement in our society can have two different outlets for girls—one through getting married and being a successful wife and mother, and the other through having a business or professional career, which usually involves a college education, as with boys.

Girls with superior intellectual ability are likely to feel a good deal of conflict at this point, and to be uncertain about their next steps after high school graduation. Thus Stivers' prediction of college-

going was not very accurate for girls, whereas it was accurate for
boys. From his interviews with able girls in the tenth grade, he
found 25 to be "non-motivated for college"; and only 3 of this group
actually entered college. But of the 38 girls whom he pronounced

TABLE 30. COMPARISON OF GIRLS WHO WENT TO COL-
LEGE WITH GIRLS WHO DID NOT (UPPER QUARTER OF
INTELLECTUAL ABILITY)

		Went to College	Did not Go to College	
High achievers in high school		18	12	$p = .02$
Low achievers in high school		8	21	
Quartile rank in high school class: school marks	IV High	22	13	
	III	2	18	$p = .001$
	II	1	1	
	I	0	1	
	Unknown	1		
Social class	A	7	2	
	B	9	17	$p = .20$
	C	10	12	
	D	0	2	
Mean T-score on California Psychological Inventory		56.2	51.9	$p = .01$

			Married	Not married	(College vs. marriage)
n-Achievement	Grade 10	7.80	9.53	6.63	$p = .3$
	Grade 12	4.58	6.86	7.07	$p = .25$

"well-motivated for college," 12, or almost a third, did not enter college. These girls probably felt some desire to go to college, but during their last two years of high school they decided that marriage and
a family were more important. Of these 12 girls, 6 were married by
the end of the year following their high school graduation.
*Characteristics of Able Girls Who Did and Who Did Not Go to
College.* The girls in Stivers' study were studied again after their
high school graduation, with results reported in Table 30. As was the
case with boys, those who got the best school grades in high school
were more likely to go to college. Also the girls who achieved best in

high school relative to their intellectual ability tended to go to college. Probably the motivation of the girls who had decided to go to college kept their school grades high, whereas others of equal ability who were not going to college demanded less of themselves in their school work.

In contrast to the boys, there was not much relation between social class and college-going among the able girls. Probably the desire for marriage and a home is about equally distributed among the various social classes, although a number of upper-middle class girls see their way clear to marrying the kind of man they want through going to college and perhaps meeting him there.

There was a reliable superiority of the college-going girls over the noncollege-going ones on the California Psychological Inventory, as was true of boys.

With respect to the measures of need for achievement, Table 30 shows the results from three groups: those who went to college, and two groups of those who did not go to college—divided into those who were married one year after high school graduation and an equal number of those who were not yet married, but were working. The results do not show any reliable differences in need for achievement among these three groups, either at the tenth or the twelfth grade level. This is similar to Stivers' findings, and suggests that a girl with a strong need for achievement has alternative channels for this need in River City.*

These various patterns of motivation are illustrated in the following reports on individual girls in the able group.

Susan. A blonde, lower-middle class girl with an extremely high n-Achievement score, Susan planned to get a secretarial job after graduation from high school. "I will work through the summer until around November. Then I plan to get married," she told the interviewer. During her earliest years in elementary school, she received only above-average marks, although some of her teachers felt that she could get top marks in all subjects if she tried. Until she entered junior high school, however, no one else set high standards for her. "In the seventh grade I started to run around with Judy. She liked to get good grades, and she was jealous of mine. I didn't care at first, but in the end I tried to beat her, and I did." Through grade school and into high school, her parents' attitude

---

* In a study which combined the data from this group of girls with data from the girls who graduated from high school in 1960, Pierce found that n-achievement, measured in the twelfth grade, of girls going to college was significantly lower than that of girls who did not go to college.

towards her marks did not change a great deal. "They're like me. They want me to get A's and B's, but if I get a C it doesn't bother them much."

Other personal influences in her life did change, though. In high school, her best friend made only average marks. Of the boy to whom she became engaged she said with a laugh, "Well, he gets average and sometimes maybe a little lower marks. He doesn't hate school or anything, but he enjoys himself while he's here." During this period, Susan was also influenced by her sister, who was taking a correspondence course in art but planned an early marriage.

Of her own plans, Susan explained: "I used to want to be an airline hostess, but no more. It's too dangerous, and I want to live. Now I want to be a secretary. Mother was a secretary for a lawyer, and the work sounds interesting to me. I like courts. I *do* know for sure that I will be married in November of the year I graduate. Whether I continue to work after that will depend on many things."

Nona. Nona, a tall, attractive, brunette, upper-lower class girl with an extremely high *n*-Achievement score, planned to "get a secretarial job here in the city. The money I earn is going to be put in the bank for a trip to Hollywood or New York, where I'll try my luck at acting," she told the interviewer.

When she was a child, mixed standards were set for her school work. Her parents expected her to do well but said very little about the matter. Her oldest sister was a good student, but the next older sister was not and finally quit school before she finished. Most of Nona's friends got average marks, and she remembers only one teacher who encouraged her. In those early years, no one influenced her to go to college. When she was about eleven years old, her life goals began to take shape. "Near the end of grade school I don't know what happened, but mother let me go places more, and I went to the show a lot. My hobby is collecting pictures of movie stars. I don't know what impressed me, but I guess it was seeing other people acting on the screen. When I saw them acting, I liked it. And I thought I could do it, too."

After she entered high school, her parents were more vocal about how well she should do. "My father, especially, is always telling me he wants me to finish school, and he wants to make sure I do. When I bring cards home and there's something I've fallen down in, he usually gets kind of mad and tells me to work harder at it because he knows I can do better."

On plans for the future, her parents offered little specific advice. "Dad never says much, but he always tells me that, when I get out of high school, I should try to get a good job. He doesn't say what kind." One of the sisters worked as a telephone operator, the other in a supermarket. Among her friends, some had plans to get a secretarial job, some to get married; some did not know what they would do. Of her own plans, she said:

"There are really two things in my mind: movies and secretarial work. You see, when I started high school, I took typing. I had always liked that sort of thing, so I made good marks and really loved it. I decided then that, since I got along so well in typing, I should be a secretary. Then in ninth grade I took speech and dramatics because it had so much to do with acting. Ever since I was old enough to go to the movies alone, I've wanted to be an actress. I'm now taking Radio Workshop and plan to take it in my next two years of school. But I'm keeping up on both my acting and secretarial work. The last I keep to fall back on if acting doesn't work out. I know acting is a difficult field. I've always thought that I'd like to work in a big office. I like to be with people and maybe with important people. I think it would help me get over my shyness. So I suppose I'll start with secretarial work and keep working and save money, then travel some and go to Hollywood to see what I can find there—something to do with acting."

The stories of two other students, Helen and Louise, illustrate how girls are influenced to aim for college and a professional career.

Helen. A pretty, upper-lower class girl with a very low n-Achievement score, Helen planned to go to college and become a teacher. When she was in elementary school, her parents never pushed her to do well, but they did maintain a steady interest in her work. "They were interested but didn't force me," she told the interviewer. "They more or less expected me to get top marks. Before the sixth grade they always wanted me to be a nurse, but when I got older, I decided I didn't want to be one, so they dropped the idea. They want me to be as successful as I want to be, but they think I'll get married and end up as a secretary. They don't discourage me, either one, much, but once my Dad told me that if I wanted to go to college bad enough, I would work for it. He said it wouldn't be fair for him to pay my way through college, and not pay for the four other sisters."

Although neither her parents nor her friends particularly encouraged her college ideas, one teacher did. "One of the most important persons in my early life was a teacher in seventh grade. We all liked him even before we got into seventh grade. He was friendly, and I talked to him often in and out of class. I used to help him with marks and things, copying marks on report cards. He seemed to think I had ability, so I didn't want to let him down. He was a good teacher, and he wanted me to be one, too."

In high school she received additional support for her plans. "This year there's a teacher that I think an awful lot of. She told me that I should be a teacher and that I could be a good one. When someone has confidence in you like that, you try harder."

About herself and her plans for the future, she said: "I think I have done OK in school so far. I haven't particularly thought about it, though. I don't know if I can be a success at it. I haven't thought too much of the practical side. I've always wanted to do the thing that would help people—humanity—the most. That's what made me want to be a nurse. And now I want to teach, probably for the same reason. It's just that it seems to me that I have some kind of obligation to society—to help people. My religion has been a great influence on me. My desire to do something worthwhile has influenced me more than people have, except maybe for my teachers. They haven't given me the idea, though. I want to go to college and be a teacher. I'm most interested in special education, and in this field the education of the mentally handicapped would probably be my choice. It is a worthwhile occupation, one in which I can be of service. Psychology interests me, too, and psychology definitely plays a part in the teaching of mentally handicapped children. I feel it is a field I can handle, something I can understand, in contrast to most scientific fields. I am also interested in missionary work. I think there are opportunities in our own country, especially in rural areas, where I could assist in missionary work and teach the mentally handicapped, too. After that I might run an orphan's home. I have always wanted to do that kind of work. I don't feel I would be doing much with my life if I spent it as a typist or a waitress. However, I do think marriage is important, and I'm not so devoted to humanity that I don't want a family of my own some day!"

Louise. Louise, a lower-middle class girl with an average n-Achievement score, planned to go to college—a teachers college. "I want to get my Master's degree and teach English," she told the interviewer. When she was a child, two of the most important people in her life were teachers. "They were sweet, wonderful persons. They expected good things of me—excellent marks—and put me in the limelight frequently." Her parents—both had been teachers —also expected her to get excellent marks. "They placed a high value on study and mentioned it often. I think my grandmother mentioned it often, too. She didn't have the opportunity to finish high school and college, and she was always sorry." This atmosphere of great expectations agreed with Louise. She worked hard and did well, pleasing her elders a great deal and getting much personal satisfaction in the process.

In high school, she found another teacher with whom to identify. "My English teacher is a wonderful person and teacher, and does what I want to do. I see my old English teacher occasionally, too, and I would like to be a teacher just like her. I know they both expect good things from me. I made almost straight A's in their classes, but I think I should. English is a natural for me. I've told them of my ambition, and they've encouraged me."

Besides this support, there was encouragement from other quarters. In her circle of best friends—all very good students—two wanted to be English teachers. Her father was very much pleased with his daughter's choice, as was her mother. "Naturally they place a high value on education. They are proud that I have never missed the honor roll, and they hope that I make National Honor Society. My mom and dad have influenced me a great deal, as have my English teachers all along the way. I admire them and hope to do the work they are doing. I know of no reason why I can't be an English teacher. Many others have made it."

Conclusions for Girls

From our study of the educational motivation of able girls, we see that some expect to combine college education with a career and marriage, others want marriage and a family without waiting to get a college education, and others want college and a career, with marriage and family postponed and possibly subordinated.

It is a question of values and personal preference which of these patterns is more desirable. If it was concluded that more girls should go to college, there would be target groups similar to those among the boys, lower-middle and upper-working class girls in the top two quartiles of intellectual ability. The top quartile alone would provide some 12 per cent of the total age group of girls who did not go to college from River City.

A campaign to recruit more of these girls for college would have much more difficulty in getting support from parents and response from girls than would a similar campaign directed at boys.

9

MARRIAGE

GIRLS ARE MORE FORTUNATE than boys in River City because a girl who finds the pathway to adulthood blocked in the school may easily find an alternative in marriage. While boys have found it increasingly difficult to get work in their midteens in recent years, girls have found it easier to get married than formerly. This is proven by the fact that the age of marriage has been decreasing in the United States since the beginning of the century, and this decrease has continued through the 1950's. Thus the median age of first marriage for women in the United States was 22 in 1900, 20.6 in 1950, and dropped below 20 by 1960.

A number of River City girls followed marriage rather than school as a pathway to adulthood. To say that they deliberately chose marriage rather than school would be accurate only in a few cases, but, as they felt their way toward adulthood, they found the school to be an obstacle, a confusing, baffling situation, while it seemed just natural for them to quit school and get married.

Of 67 girl dropouts, 52 were married by the age of 18, and only 8 were left unmarried in December, 1960, when nearly everybody in the study group was 20 or more.

Among the total River City group, an even 50 per cent of the girls were married before they were 20 years old. Six girls were married at 14 or 15; 20 at 16; 28 at 17; 38 at 18; and 26 at 19. Although the ages of 14, 15, and 16 were considered somewhat young for marriage, a number of these girls were simply repeating the example set by

119

their own mothers. Table 31 shows that girls who dropped out of school were likely to marry shortly afterward. Indeed, marriage or pregnancy was the cause of many of these dropouts. By the age of sixteen, marriage was generally approved, and eighteen was the age at which the largest number of girls were married. It was the expected thing for a considerable group of girls to graduate from high school and then marry during the following months.

Boys marry later than girls. Only 6 boys were married at seventeen or younger, compared with 54 girls. This ratio of 9 to 1 is exactly the ratio for marriages in England through the age of eighteen. But

TABLE 31. AGE AT SCHOOL DROPOUT AND AGE AT MARRIAGE (GIRLS)

Age at School Dropout	Under 16	16	17	18	19	20	21	Not by Dec. '60	Total
Under 16	6	3	2	0	0	0	0	0	11
16 to 16½	0	13	4	0	0	2	1	4	24
16½ and over	0	4	13	7	3	1	0	4	32
									67

Age at Marriage

when marriages of eighteen-year-olds are included in the figures from River City, the ratio drops to about 3 to 1, for a considerable number of boys were married at eighteen.

Social Class, Intelligence, and Early Marriage

Table 32 shows how social class and age of marriage are related for those who married early. Three-fourths of the Class D girls were married by the age of 20, and 43 per cent were married before reaching the age of 18. On the other hand, only one-fourth of the Class A girls were married by twenty. There is no clear relation of social class to age of marriage among the boys, except that none of the Class A boys was married before the age of 19.

Table 33 shows the expected relationship between intelligence and age of marriage. Girls in the lower half of the group in intelligence are much more likely to marry early than are girls in the upper half. Boys do not show this relationship as much as girls. It is only the

TABLE 32. SOCIAL CLASS AND AGE AT MARRIAGE
(FOR THOSE MARRIED BY DECEMBER 1, 1960)

Age at Marriage	Girls					Boys				
	A	B	C	D	Total	A	B	C	D	Total
Under 16	0	0	2	4	6	0	0	0	0	0
16	1	2	7	10	20	0	0	0	1	1
17	0	6	12	10	28	0	1	3	1	5
18	2	9	18	9	38	0	4	12	4	20
19	3	12	6	5	26	1	6	7	11	25
20	0	5	10	3	18	2	3	7	7	19
21–22	0	0	0	1	1	0	0	5	1	6
Total number	6	34	55	42	137	3	14	34	25	76
Per cent of social-class group	27	55	59	72	58	14	22	37	37	32

Note: The entire cohort was 19 or more by December, 1960. Therefore the only ages that can receive later additions are those from 20 on.

TABLE 33. INTELLIGENCE QUOTIENT AND AGE AT
MARRIAGE (FOR THOSE MARRIED BY DECEMBER 1, 1960)

Age at Marriage	Girls IQ Quartile						Boys IQ Quartile					
	(high) IV	III	II	I	Un-known	Total	IV	III	II	I	Un-known	Total
Under 16	0	1	3	1	1	6	0	0	0	0	0	0
16	1	3	6	10	0	20	0	0	0	1	0	1
17	5	7	9	7	0	28	0	3	1	1	0	5
18	11	8	10	8	1	38	2	7	6	5	0	20
19	10	5	8	3	0	26	3	7	7	8	0	25
20	3	3	7	5	0	18	2	5	6	5	1	19
21–22	0	0	0	0	1	1	0	1	0	5	0	6
Total number	30	27	43	34	3	137	7	23	20	25	1	76
Per cent of IQ group	48	47	66	63		58	15	37	30	40		32

Note: The entire cohort was 19 or more by December, 1960. Therefore the only ages that can receive later additions are those from 20 on.

boys in the upper quarter of intelligence who seem to marry later than the others.

The Quality of the Early Marriages

Some of the early marriages give every indication of being good, stable ones, while others got off to a bad start. One of the girls was married for only two weeks, and then got a divorce. Another got a divorce after living with her husband for only two months. She had a baby by this husband, and has since married a man in the army. Two girls had husbands in prison when the girls were 18. Both girls had babies. One was sueing for divorce, while the other was thinking about it.

The following interviews will show the differences between a good and a poor marriage in this group. Sandra Miller, who was married before she was 16, seems to have gotten off to a good start. But Patricia Maxwell, married at 17, has made a poor beginning.

The interviews show that each girl had come to a dead end in school. In order to grow up, they left school and launched into matrimony—a course which was open and attractive to them.

Patricia. Patricia Maxwell is a Class D girl, one of six children in a family that is well known to the police and the social agencies. The father is an odd-jobs man and frequently abandons the family, while the mother works occasionally as a dishwasher. The family started in a small rural village and moved to River City when Patricia was in elementary school.

Patricia quit school three days after her sixteenth birthday and worked at various places until her pregnancy caused her to stop working. She was involved with several boys, and married George Moore near the time of her seventeenth birthday. Both Patricia and her husband were very poor students in school. They were interviewed by a man who was selected for his ability to get along well with people who might be suspicious or hostile. His report of the interview follows:

Patricia lives in depressing surroundings in a tenement apartment with her mother and other members of the family. An older pregnant sister was sitting in the front yard when I called. She directed me around to the rear of the house where the "yard" was full of busted bottles and filthy boxes. The mother was hanging out laundry here. She told me that Patricia wasn't feeling well and was in bed this morning. She said Patricia is pregnant and it is

bothering her quite a bit.   I prepared to leave saying that I would
return, when George (Patricia's husband) hailed me through one
of the cracked windows as I walked around the house.   Mrs.
Maxwell then went in to investigate to see if Patricia was up.   In a
few minutes Pat came out to the front porch looking very tired and
very weak.   Suddenly a large group of adolescents of various ages
gathered around us, most of them junior high age, a few younger,
all of them trying to mooch a cigarette off of someone.   Several of
them stayed a few minutes and exchanged a few words and then
wandered on.   There seemed to be a large number of little children.
Patricia's husband, George, came out and made a few comments
about school.   He then hopped on a bicycle telling his wife he
would see her later.   I asked Patricia just when she quit school.

"I quit two or three weeks before school was out a year ago."

"Was that when you turned sixteen?"

"Yes, that's right."

"How long have you been married?"

"Two weeks."

"What did you do during the time since you left school?"

"I worked a little while at different places.   I worked at the Old
People's Home for three weeks, the Quality Cafe for about a week
or so, and at the Shoe Factory for a month or maybe two months."

"Which job did you like the best?"

"I liked the Quality Cafe job.   I was waiting tables.   I made 75
cents an hour there and a little bit on tips.   They aren't very big
there though."

"What kind of work can a young girl get in this town?"

"It's hard to get a job.   I looked and looked for a month or so,
then I got that job at the Home.   That was nerve-racking.   I was
supposed to carry trays but I did about everything else."

"Were they rather strict at these places you worked, about taking
a day off, or coming in late?"

"Oh, yes, they were.   At the Quality Cafe, I was sick one day and
didn't go to work.   I went back and they said, "We won't need you
anymore."   I had even telephoned them and told them I couldn't
come in."

"Pat, when you quit school, were most of your friends in or out of
school?"

"They were mostly in."

"How about now?"

"A lot are out now."

"What would you say the main reason was for your quitting
school?"

"I couldn't get along with teachers. That was the main reason. I really didn't like any of them. Brown was the only one I could get along with. Me and Muller, we always got into it. French was all right until she tried to pick my friends. I was running around with my husband's sister, Sally Moore, and she told me I could find somebody better than that to pal around with. I said, 'Look here, you can be my teacher, but you aren't going to pick my friends'."

"In what way, Pat, is being out better for you than being in school?"

"In a way it seems better and in a way it don't. When you are in school, at least you have some place to go and pass the time."

"Were there any subjects that you had that you really liked in the ninth grade?"

"I didn't learn anything. I didn't study much in any subject."

"Pat, how did your friends feel about the social life at Junior High School, the basketball games and dances?"

"I think most of them went to the dances."

"How did you feel about them?"

"I went to about three school dances."

"Do you and your husband have any plans for the future? Do you plan to stay here with your mother?"

"Yes, we will stay here until the baby comes."

"Pat, I guess it is pretty hard for George to find work."

"He can't find anything and I couldn't work now either. I am so dizzy on being pregnant."

"How long have you been married now?"

"Two weeks."

"Pat, if you had to do things over again, would you continue in school or drop school?"

"I would still quit."

"Pat, would you say that Junior High was much harder than grade school?"

"Well, no. I probably could have passed if I tried. But I never did try. When I listened to something I could get it. But I never listened for anything except the buzzer for the end of the period."

Although the relation between Patricia and her husband does not appear to be bad, in this interview, it is clear that there is no adequate economic basis for this marriage. The boy husband is not supporting his wife, and neither is he studying so that he will be able to support her later. The marriage of Sandra has a better economic base.

Sandra.   Sandra Miller is a Class C girl of about average intelligence. She quit school at the end of the tenth grade and was married that month, before she was sixteen.   Her husband was three years older and was working as an apprentice electrician.   The interviewer's report follows.

Sandra and her husband have a year-and-a-half-old baby and live in a small unpretentious frame house.   Sandra was frank about herself and said she had to quit school after the tenth grade and get married because she was pregnant.   Sandra mentioned several times during our talk that they didn't have a very fancy place, but that everything they had was their own.   She said that they didn't believe in buying things until they had the money to pay for them.   She also said that someday Earl (her husband) will be making good money and things will be a little better.   She seems happily married and is expecting another youngster.   Sandra has not had any working experience.

"Of course, I was going with Earl all that time I was in high school.   I started going with him when I was 13.   I liked Home Economics and Biology.   But I couldn't understand English and Arithmetic.   I still don't know the difference between verbs and adverbs and all of that.   And I can't add or subtract, either one, yet. The only things that come easy for me are taking care of kids and cooking.   That's a lot better than working eight hours in a factory."

"As you look back on things, what was your main reason for leaving school?"

"To get married.   Ever since I was little, I remember wanting to get married and have a home and kids of my own.   I remember telling my mom when I was a little girl that I wanted 20 kids.   I think I changed my mind about that now."

"If you had it to do over again, and things were about the same, would you quit or go on to school?"

"Yes, I'd quit, if I was going with Earl.   I know I would."

"You are not sorry you quit school then?"

"No, I'm not.   I didn't like school that much."

At the end of the interview, Sandra talked about feeling dumb in class and I asked her just how she felt.   She said, "I felt like when a teacher called on me and I would stand up and give the answer it would be wrong and the kids would laugh at me.   I always did have an inferiority complex.   At least that's what the doctor calls it."

"Maybe you just thought you had one."

"Well, you ought to see me shake."

Ratings of Marriages. There were 149 marriages in the study group before November 1959, with 106 girls and 43 boys as principals. These will be called "early marriages," since they all occurred at the age of 19 or under, and most of them at 18 or younger. To gain a general idea of the quality of these marriages, a crude rating was made, on a five-point scale. Two women and two men on the staff did the rating. The women were married and had been living in River City for some time. They know some of the boys and girls personally. The highest ratings were given to couples who appeared to be getting along fairly well and were obviously well mated in terms of cultural and religious background. In most cases there were interviews with the husband or wife, during which comments were made concerning satisfaction or dissatisfaction with the marriage relationship, devotion to husband or wife, and so on.

At the low end of the scale were placed marriages where there was evidence of quarreling and threatened separation, application or plans for divorce, desertion, husband in jail, or evidence of sexual promiscuity of either partner since marriage. In addition, marriages were rated low where the relatives complained about the marriage, where either partner had been engaged in delinquent acts since marriage, and where the girl was pregnant at the time of the marriage unless the couple had been engaged for some time prior to the marriage. Ratings in the middle level were given to those marriages which were all right as far as could be seen but about which there was not much information.

The ratings were very similar for boys and for girls. When the age of the girl or boy at marriage was compared with the marriage rating, as seen in Table 34, there was a tendency for higher ratings to be associated with the later ages. A chi-square test of the difference between the marrigaes at 17 or below and those at 18 and 19 indicates this difference to be statistically significant at the .1 level, indicating that the tendency is not a strong one.

Educational progress is clearly related to success of marriage, as is seen in Table 35. Comparing school dropouts with high school graduates and those who attended college, the dropouts had much lower marriage ratings. The chi-square test shows the difference to be significant at the .01 level.

However, it is not intelligence that controls the success of the marriage as much as social class. Among the early-marrying girls who were in Class C or D and also in the lower half of the total group in intelligence, the success ratings show a large difference between classes C and D in favor of the upper-lower as against the lower-

lower class. At the same time there is not a reliable difference between those in the two quartiles of intelligence, as can be seen in
Table 9-1 in the Appendix.

The group who were married early were more likely than the still
unmarried ones to come from homes broken by death, desertion, or

TABLE 34. SUCCESS OF MARRIAGE RELATED TO AGE
AT MARRIAGE (BOYS AND GIRLS)

AGE OF MARRIAGE

Rating of Marriage	Before 16	16	17	18	19+	Total
5 (high)	1	4	7	24	9	45
4	1	3	3	10	5	22
3	0	5	8	7	7	27
2	0	2	7	5	1	15
1 (low)	3	6	6	10	9	34
No information	1	0	3	1	1	6
Total	6	20	34	57	32	149
Mean rating	2.40	2.85	2.94	3.59	3.13	3.20

TABLE 35. SUCCESS OF MARRIAGE RELATED TO
EDUCATIONAL ATTAINMENT (BOYS AND GIRLS)

Rating of Marriage	Drop out in grade:				Hi. Sch. Grad.	Hi. Sch. plus	One yr. College Success	No Info.	Total
	7-9	10	11	12					
5 (high)	1	3	2	4	31	2	2	0	45
4	1	5	2	2	10	1	1	0	22
3	7	1	8	0	10	1	0	0	27
2	5	2	2	4	1	0	0	1	15
1	16	6	6	1	4	1	0	0	34
No info.	2	1	0	0	1	0	0	2	6
Total	32	18	20	11	57	5	3	3	149
Mean rating	1.87	2.82	2.60	3.36	4.12	3.60	4.67	—	3.20

divorce. Only 57 per cent of the married ones opposed to 72 per
cent of those still unmarried came from homes in which both parents
were living with each other. Table 9-2 in the Appendix shows that
among the group already married there was a tendency for the more
successful marriages to be made by boys and girls whose own parents

were alive and living together. The chi-square test is significant at
the 1 per cent level.

The Kind of Girl or Boy Who Marries Early

There is a tendency for girls and boys of lower intelligence and
lower social class to marry early, although there are many exceptions
to this tendency. There is also a tendency for those with poor social
adjustment to marry early, as is shown in Table 9-3 in the Appendix.

The social adjustment scores for grades 6 and 7, or those for grade
9 in case earlier ones were not available, were averaged for the girls
who were married before January 5, 1959, and for the boys who were
married before November 1959.

For girls, the results are as follows: the girls who married at 18 or
19 did not differ from the total group of girls in social adjustment.
However, the girls who married at 17 or before had lower scores in
social leadership and higher scores in withdrawal than the total group.

For the boys, those few who married at 17 or before had strong
maladjustment scores, and the larger number who married at 18 or 19
had lower leadership scores and higher aggression scores than the total
group.

Looking at the girls with very high scores for maladjustment in the
sixth and seventh grades, we see that they were especially likely to
marry early. Of 16 girls in the top 10 per cent for aggressive maladjustment, 9 dropped out of school and were married, and a tenth was
married as soon as she graduated from high school. Sixteen out of
30 girls in the top 10 per cent for withdrawn maladjustment were
married early, 10 of them dropping out of school and 6 graduating
from high school. This at least indicates that being "withdrawn"
socially at the sixth grade did not handicap a girl for early marriage.
Church Relationship and Early Marriage. There was a strong
tendency for early-marrying youth to have little contact with the
church, as is shown in Table 36. Of 78 girls who were married at 18
or younger, 31 were not known to a clergyman, 22 were known but the
church was unimportant to them, and 25 were seen by the clergy as
finding the church to be important. Among the 32 boys who married
earliest, 20 were not known to a clergyman and only 7 were reported
as finding importance in the church.
Girls Who Marry Early. What kind of girl marries early? It appears
that there are two types. One type is a C or D Class girl who is
socially maladjusted in school and is doing poor school work. For

this kind of girl, whose progress is blocked along the lines she sees her classmates following who have more social prestige and more academic success, marriage is the best solution. It is a chance at something she wants and vaguely imagines, though the reality may be different from what she expects.

Marriage is the only constructive behavior of which this type of girl is capable. Too often, she cannot support this role effectively, and no one is there to help her. But it works frequently enough, as in the case of Sandra Miller, to make it a possibility that parents and advisers must recognize.

TABLE 36. EARLY MARRIAGE AND CHURCH PARTICIPATION

Age of Marriage	Church is Important		Known to Ch. but Ch. is unimportant		Unknown to Church	
	M	F	M	F	M	F
−16	0	1	0	0	0	5
16	0	4	1	8	0	10
17	0	12	2	5	1	9
18	7	8	2	9	9	7
19	0	—	0	—	10	—
Total no.	7	25	5	22	20	31

The other type of girl who marries early is a Class B, C or D girl who gets along quite well in school but prefers marriage immediately after high school graduation to going to college or starting a career. For this girl, high school has been a satisfactory pathway to growing up, but marriage is the desirable course as soon as high school is completed. Some of the talented girls are in this group: 5 of 34 in the intellectually talented group, 3 of 37 in the leadership group, and 2 of 29 in the group showing artistic talent.

Boys Who Marry Early. Most of the boys who marry at 18 or before are dropouts, whose school record was poor and whose social adjustment in school was poor. For them, marriage sometimes has a stabilizing effect. Others, however, cannot carry the responsibility and fail in this as well as in work. A small group of boys are analogous to the second group of girls who have just been described. They have done fairly well in school, and upon graduation from high school they go to work and get married, thus moving into adulthood in a serious and responsible way.

The Social Desirability of Early Marriage

It is clear that the statistical chances of success are less for an early marriage than for one at 18 or later for girls and 20 or later for boys. However, there are some very successful early marriages. It is more true to say that the people with the poorest chance of making a good marriage are most likely to marry early, than to say that early marriage causes failure in marriage. There is no evidence that these people would make better marriages if they waited to marry for three or four years beyond their present rather early age. It is also very likely that a wise adult could select a group of 16-year-old girls and 18-year-old boys who would make successful marriages if they were to marry early. And a few such young people did marry early in River City, and have been successful with their marriages.

From the point of view of the individual girl who is failing in school, the most desirable thing is likely to be an early marriage. From society's point of view, it would be better if this type of girl was better prepared for marriage and for adult life, for it seems clear that under present conditions these girls will marry early unless a much more attractive alternative course is open to them, and no such alternative has been offered them by society.

10

≈≈≈

WORK

IN RIVER CITY the achievement of a stable responsible job is the principal sign of maturity for a young person. Not until he has made this achievement is he regarded as a responsible adult. The only exception to this rule is found in girls who marry early and make a success of marriage. Boys and girls who go to college are understood to have postponed the task of establishing themselves as workers in the adult society, though they have a good chance of making an outstanding success of their work by getting a college education.

The age of achievement of a responsible work role varies from as young as 16 for a rare youth to as old as 30 for a youth who must follow an extensive training program for several years beyond college graduation in such a field as medicine, mathematics, or law.

Work experience itself is a part of the growing-up process for most young people. They learn habits of character as well as vocational skills while actively on the job. For noncollege youth, work experience is a kind of informal apprenticeship lasting one to five years. College youth come to their first full-time job with more maturity, but still they have much to learn from their work experience.

This chapter deals with achievement and lack of achievement in the work area by all except the "successful" college group—those who have continued in college beyond the first year and therefore have no work record that can be studied—and the girls who entered a

131

school of nursing and were still in training when the study was made. The ones who dropped out of college during the first year are included in this report. Girls who never entered the working force (most of them having married early) are also omitted from this study.

Questions to be answered are: What kinds of work experience and work adjustment do high school dropouts have in comparison to high school graduates? How much influence do intelligence, socioeconomic status, and personal-social adjustment have on work adjustment? What work-experience opportunities does River City offer to its youth at various ages? To what extent does the school assist young people in their work adjustment? To what degree is work a feasible pathway of growth to adulthood?

Methods of Studying Work Experience and Work Adjustment

Two somewhat related concepts were used in the study of work. One was the *Job Category* of a youth at the time of the study, the autumn and winter of 1959–1960, when most of the boys and girls were 19 years old. The other was the *Work Adjustment* of a boy or girl, which took into account the total work experience of the person to date, and was aimed at measuring his achievement of the task of getting started in a work career.

Job Category. Current jobs of the members of the study were classified into four categories, moving from the least desirable jobs (including unemployment for those who were still seeking work) to the most desirable. The categories were:

1. No work experience or unemployed more than half the time since leaving school.
    Occasional odd jobs for predetermined short periods.
    Manual labor with no job security.
2. Unskilled manual labor with fairly good job security.
    Low-paying semiskilled jobs with little job security or opportunity for advancement. (These jobs require no previous education, training, or experience; there are few fringe benefits.)
3. Semiskilled job in a fairly stable or stable industry or business. Opportunity for pay increases through seniority, but few opportunities for promotion (such jobs as file clerk in an office or poorly paid white-collar jobs such as ten-cent-store clerks fall in this category).
    Military service—routine assignment not involving a marketable skill.

(In general, the jobs in this category have the advantage of stability and the disadvantage of being blind alleys that do not lead to promotion.

4. Skilled job or one which leads fairly directly to a skilled job.

Job involving a marketable skill with opportunity at least for limited advancement (bookkeepers, secretaries, electrician apprentices, etc., fall in this category)

Military service—special training in a marketable skill and advances in rating.

Work Adjustment. This is a rating of the individual rather than the job, and refers to his past work experience as well as his attitudes and performance in his present job. This rating depended considerably upon the employer's report, which was obtained through an interview in which the employer was asked whether he would like to keep this person as a permanent employee and what he saw as the occupational future for this person. The rating also depended on what the individual said about his job, in an interview sometimes made in person and sometimes by telephone, or in a brief questionnaire that was filled out and mailed in by the boy or girl. Other information serving as a basis for the Work-Adjustment rating as well as the Job-Category rating came from interviews held with all school-dropouts four to six months after they quit school. The ratings were given by two staff members working independently. After they had finished their ratings they compared notes and where they had disagreed they discussed each case and agreed upon a rating.

The categories or points on the scale of *Work Adjustment* were defined as follows:

1. Seldom does satisfactory work.
   Doesn't care what happens to him job-wise.
   Holds jobs for short times and is discharged.
   Chronically unemployed or has not worked although not in school and (for a girl) not married.
2. Chronic complainer, employer regards him as a malcontent; finds no job or working conditions to his liking.
   Holds jobs longer than those rated 1 but eventually quits, is discharged, or is regarded as an undesirable employee by his employer.
   Getting nowhere in a work career.
3. Steady, stable, but limited.
   Relatively satisfied with work of this type and will likely stay on here indefinitely, or will take a similar job elsewhere.

No particular drive to get ahead.

May have doubts about the future occupationally, but meanwhile is doing an adequate job where he is.

4. Can expect limited advancement into supervisory or skilled job. Is moving ahead largely through seniority.

Likes his work.

May have shifted jobs but each time has bettered his position with either better pay or more opportunities for advancement.

5. The individual has realistic plans for advancement in the future accompanied by realistic actions in the present.

His employer thinks he will advance to a position of responsibility in the company.

Happy in his work.

Has learned from every work experience, has a flair for this kind of work, feels comfortable in it, and is sure of promotions to a very responsible job.

There is a high correlation ($r = .79$) between Work Adjustment and Job Category, but the two concepts are so different that it seems useful to treat them separately.

Jobs and School Achievement

A youth's present job is obviously related to his educational attainment, as can be seen in Table 37. This table has been worked out for 255 boys and girls, and excludes all those attending colleges or schools of nursing, as well as girls who married early and were never really in the working force. It includes 255 persons, 115 girls and 140 boys, and is similar in persons included, to the other tables in this chapter.

The best jobs are held almost without exception by high school graduates, while the dropouts hold the poorest jobs or are unemployed. There is also a steady progression to better jobs among the dropouts from those dropping out earliest to those staying in school longest. This is despite the fact that dropouts have been in the labor market longer than high school graduates, and earlier dropouts have been in the labor market longer than those who dropped out at eleventh or twelfth grade.

Another indication of the close relationship between school achievement and work achievement is seen in Table 38, which shows the relation of job category to class rank in the eleventh grade. The lower one goes in class rank the lower one goes in job category.

Since dropouts generally have lower intelligence than high school graduates, and for this reason alone might get poorer jobs, we have compared dropouts with graduates who were matched with them in IQ and social class as described in Chapter 5.

TABLE 37. JOB CATEGORY AND EDUCATIONAL CAREER

Job Category

Educational Career	4 (high)	3	2	1	Total
Beyond high school	7	6	1	0	14
High school graduate	24	85	18	6	133
Dropped 12th grade	1	9	8	2	20
Dropped 11th grade	1	10	10	5	26
Dropped 10th grade	0	9	11	5	25
Dropped 9, 8, 7th grades	1	7	15	14	37
Total	34	126	63	32	255

Note: This table excludes those attending college or schools of nursing.

TABLE 38. JOB CATEGORY VS. RANK IN HIGH-SCHOOL CLASS ELEVENTH GRADE

Rank in High School Class (Quartiles)	Job Category				Total	Mean Score
	4 (high)	3	2	1		
IV (high)	9	9	1	0	19	3.42
III	12	18	5	1	36	3.14
II	7	31	7	2	47	2.91
I	3	33	11	5	52	2.65
Total	31	91	24	8	154	2.94

Both controls and dropouts reported considerable difficulty in finding jobs for young people, and the jobs available fell into a relatively narrow range. The best job obtained by any dropout was one of working in a real estate office and it lasted only one month. Three girls of the control group found clerical jobs in business offices, two control boys became apprentice mechanics, and one control boy gave private music lessons in a music store. These were all given ratings of four.

The poorest jobs, those rated one, included bus boy, dishwasher, service station attendant, clean-up work, delivery boy, pinsetter, and odd manual-labor jobs.

The number three ratings included clerks in stores, semiskilled jobs on production lines, receptionists, cashiers, painter, and the armed services.

In Table 39, dropouts and controls are compared on the kinds of jobs in which they were employed. Almost half of the dropouts held the lowest category jobs; more than half of the controls held category-two jobs. Although those who graduated from high school were getting better jobs than the dropouts, still neither group was getting very

TABLE 39. JOB CATEGORY: DROPOUTS VS. CONTROLS (PERCENTAGES)

Job Ratings	At time of interview		At time of follow-up	
	Dropout	Control	Dropout	Control
1 (Low)	48.4	18.7	24.5	7.1
2	36.4	57.0	42.5	19.1
3	14.4	18.7	30.8	58.3
4 (High)	.8	5.6	2.2	15.5

good jobs. A follow-up of both groups was made one year later, and those results are seen in Table 39 also. It shows some improvement in both groups, with the control group in a superior position. Furthermore, the 84 persons in the control group do not include 21 who are in college, and it may be assumed that the better jobs eventually obtained by the college group will make even greater differences between dropouts and controls.

Thus, a group of high-school graduates, even when equated for intelligence and socioeconomic status, obtain considerably better jobs on the average than their peers who drop out of high school.

The dropout is clearly at a great disadvantage in the job market, and perhaps not so much because of low intelligence as because of the defects of character and motivation which caused him to drop out of school. These personality defects were seen in the chapter "Progress through School" (Chapter 5). Apparently the dropout takes his personality with him when he leaves school and this causes him to have difficulties in the world of work.

This can be seen again in the groups with the higher sixth and seventh grade maladjustment scores that were described in Chapter 3.

Only two of the highly aggressive girls and none of the boys had jobs in the most desirable category, whereas 62 per cent of them as opposed to 34 per cent of the remainder of the group had jobs in the lower two categories. The youths with high withdrawal scores were only half as likely as the remainder to have jobs in the fourth category, and they were twice as likely as the remainder to have jobs in the lowest category.

Work Adjustment and Its Correlates

Work adjustment at about the age of 19 is related to educational career as shown in Table 40. The major part of those with a high

TABLE 40. WORK ADJUSTMENT VS. EDUCATIONAL CAREER

Work Adjustment Rating

Educational Career	5,4	3	2	1	Total
Beyond high school	7	5	2	0	14
High school graduate	49	60	19	5	133
Dropped 12th grade	3	9	5	3	20
Dropped 11th grade	1	15	7	3	26
Dropped 10th grade	2	12	7	4	25
Dropped 9–7 grades	1	13	9	14	37
Total	63	114	49	29	255

Note: This table excludes those attending college or schools of nursing.

rating (4 or 5) on work adjustment have graduated from high school.

The prediction of work adjustment can be made with substantial statistical reliability from IQ at the sixth grade, and from socioeconomic status, as can be seen in Tables 41 and 42. Other prediction factors for work adjustment are seen in Table 43, where the high work-adjustment group (scores 4 and 5) is contrasted with the low work-adjustment group (score of 1).

Prediction of initial adult work adjustment can then be made for those who do not go to college on the basis of several childhood background factors, including intelligence, social status, personal-social adjustment, and family stability.

In contrast to *background* factors with which the child is mainly endowed by his family, there are *performance* factors for which he, himself, is more responsible. The performance factors come to the fore in adolescence, where one sees correlates of work adjustment with delinquency, high-school dropout, high-school class rank, personal-adjustment scores, and even in marriage, where it appears that those who marry earliest, (girls or boys) tend to make a poorer work adjustment than those who remain single until 19 or 20.

TABLE 41. WORK ADJUSTMENT VS. SIXTH GRADE INTEL-LIGENCE QUOTIENT

| 6th Grade IQ | Work Adjustment | | | | |
	5, 4	3	2	1	Total
Quartile IV (high)	19	14	4	1	38
Quartile III	16	24	5	3	48
Quartile II	20	36	16	8	80
Quartile I	6	33	22	10	71
Total	61	107	47	22	237

TABLE 42. WORK ADJUSTMENT VS. PARENTAL SOCIAL CLASS

| Parental Social Status | Work Adjustment | | | | |
	5, 4	3	2	1	Total
A (high)	3	2	1	0	6
B	18	31	6	5	60
C	32	48	23	11	114
D	10	35	19	14	78
Total	63	116	49	30	258

Cases of Good and Poor Work Adjustment

To give a more coherent and concrete description of the qualities in a person and his environment that make for good or poor work adjustment, the following three illustrative cases are presented.

Dennis. Dennis had at least five jobs during the first year after he was graduated from high school. He worked in two restaurants, a downtown store, delivered handbills, and worked in a factory. Most of these jobs lasted less than two weeks, and none lasted more

than two months.   When interviewed in August of 1959, Dennis was
unemployed.

One of Dennis's restaurant employers said of him, "The boy didn't
do any work.   He said he needed work, too.   Of course, he was all
right if you stood over him, but we couldn't do that.   We had to let

TABLE 43. COMPARISON OF HIGH AND LOW WORK
ADJUSTMENT GROUPS (PERCENTAGES TO BE FOUND IN
EACH OF THE TWO CONTRASTING GROUPS)

	High ($N = 63$)	Low ($N = 30$)
Background Factors (6th & 7th grades)		
Boys	44	67
Parents divorced or separated	6	30
Aggressive priority list	5	37
Withdrawn priority list	8	20
Talent priority lists	38	3
Personal and Social Adjustment		
(California Test of Personality)		
Quartile IV (high)	26	7
III	26	13
II	24	27
I	24	53
Performance Factors (in Adolescence)		
Personal Adjustment		
(10th grade California Psychological		
Inventory)		
Quartile IV (high)	19	0
III	29	25
II	40	12
I	12	63
Married	22	45
Delinquency levels I, II, III	11	47
High school dropout	11	83

him go after a couple of weeks."   In speaking of this job Dennis
said that he didn't stay because they didn't have enough help and
he had to stay on his feet all the time.   He said that he would have
stayed at the downtown store because it wasn't too hard, but "my
boss was a woman and I just couldn't take any more of her sass."

The supervisor at Dennis's last job, a factory job, said that he was
an extremely poor worker.   "His work was not satisfactory and we

definitely won't rehire him." Dennis says of this job. "I've been laid off at the plant, but I haven't really been looking for work lately. I don't know what I want. I've been waiting for some literature I sent away for about an electronics school. If it doesn't cost too much I might sell my car and raise the money to take the course, but I don't know."

Dennis's father was present at the interview. He said that Dennis couldn't wash dishes at the restaurant because it was too much of a strain on his bad heart. He said, "These days most employers expect too much out of young fellows. They have to work too hard when they go on jobs."

When asked what he did for recreation, Dennis said he had been playing tennis once in a while, but other than that he had just been riding around in his car. Dennis summed up his own case when he said, "I haven't amounted to much yet. I invested all my money in a car and wrecked it. Then I had to buy a junker."

This boy had somewhat below-average intellectual ability and was seen by his teachers and classmates as somewhat withdrawn. He graduated from high school near the bottom of his class. All of the self-reporting personality tests agreed that his personal and social adjustment is near the bottom of his group.

On the job, Dennis has continued the pattern he began in school, a pattern of getting by with as little work as possible. It seems likely that his father is unconsciously encouraging this behavior, and thus far there is little indication that he is learning much from his failure experiences. His high school diploma has helped him get jobs, but it has not guaranteed him success in the work world.

Linda. Linda also finished high school. She had a C— average. Until she was graduated Linda had always gotten her spending money from her parents except for occasional baby-sitting jobs. She never had many friends and was seen by her teachers and classmates as shy. In the eleventh grade she told an interviewer, "I'd like to quit school, but I don't think I'd better." When the interviewer asked, "Why?" she replied, "The diploma. Without it you wouldn't be able to get any kind of a job."

When she graduated Linda looked for work. She found a job at a drive-in restaurant. Her employer kept her for the summer season, but said of her, "She needs improvement badly! She was sloppy, often made mistakes, and acted like a 'sourpuss.' I wouldn't have her again."

For the past year Linda has been sitting around home. She has no plans for the future and doesn't belong to any social groups. She dates occasionally and reads a great deal.   Thus far she seems to be making very little contribution to society.   Her initial work experience was unpleasant, and as long as her parents will protect her from life, she intends to stay at home.   The one thing she really enjoys is taking care of children.   Perhaps she will find some fulfillment if she gets married.

David.   When he was in high school David said, "My dad helps load the trucks and those guys in the office where he works—they make pretty good money.   They sit in there and have air conditioning. I thought to myself, I would like to have a nice job like that.   I have always been good at arithmetic so I think I will go into book-keeping or accounting."   Many boys David's age dream a dream like this, but David has found a way to make his dream a reality. He has found fulfillment in work.

David didn't have a very good beginning.   He comes from a Class C family.   He has only average intellectual ability, and did good, but not outstanding, work in high school.   During his junior high school years David was arrested several times for shoplifting, but in his time of trouble the family stood by him, and a successful working experience proved to be a fine rehabilitation program.

While still in high school David began to work in a supermarket evenings and on weekends.   Here he was regarded as a good worker and as a responsible person.   When he left high school he got a job in an automobile service station.   When he talked to the interviewer about this job he commented on the fact that both the people he worked for and his customers were very pleasant.   He said, "We keep the place clean so people will want to come back; I think we sell as much gas as any other station in town."

Although David liked his job at the service station, he saw that the advancement possibilities were limited and he began to look for a better job.   He enrolled in bookkeeping and accounting at night school.   College did not appeal to him.   He says of his night-school experience, "This course is shorter, you get more done in a shorter time.   I don't want to go to college for four years.   I like to work, and I think I am moving ahead.   The course I am taking will help me on the job."   His night school teacher said that David is the kind of boy that makes use of everything he has ever learned.

Soon after enrolling in night school David got a job as a machine operator in a factory.   Four months later his employer stated that he already had advanced to a supervisory job and was doing an excellent job, "We want to keep David and we feel that he will go a long way.   He accomplishes whatever must be done."

Successful job experiences have made a big difference in David's life. Aggressiveness in school and his delinquent behavior seemed to foretell a non-productive adulthood. But David's family was able to forgive and forget his delinquency, and after successful experiences in unskilled work David seems headed toward a white-collar work career and a successful adulthood.

Conclusions

The most striking fact emerging from this survey of the work experience of River City youth is the difference in work adjustment and in job opportunities between high school graduates and high school dropouts. Just as they were more successful in school, the high school graduates are more successful in the area of work outside of school.

Thus, instead of finding work to be an alternative pathway to the school for growth to adulthood, we face the stubborn fact that work and school are sections of the same pathway, and a poor school record tends strongly to guarantee a poor work record.

There are a few interesting and important exceptions to this rule. Roy Cranston, whom we saw in the chapter on delinquency, was a failure in school but found a sure road to maturity through work.

Perhaps something could be done to carve out an alternative pathway to adulthood through work experience for those who do not learn or profit from school. In order to do this, it appears that two things would have to be accomplished that do not now exist in River City, or in other cities in the United States.

First, there is need for a substantial group of juvenile jobs, with appropriate pay and appropriate expectation of juvenile immaturity. Modern American society does not offer such jobs in anything like the quantity needed. At present almost nobody under age 15 is employed except on the home farm. Employment at ages 16 and 17 is only about half of what it was fifty years ago. Because of restrictive child labor laws, restrictive labor union policies, and restrictive employment policies, the larger business houses and industries do not employ boys and girls below the ages of 17 or 18, and the only jobs available to the high school dropout are blind-alley jobs as baby-sitters, delivery boys, service station attendants, waitresses, etc.

Not in River City and not in other cities is there an active conscience among employers concerning their responsibility for aiding in the growing-up process of youth by providing work experiences that are conducive to growth for those who need it most—the boys and girls who are not successful in growing up through school.

II

EARLY ADULT STATUS
AND SOCIAL MOBILITY

A MERICAN DEMOCRACY has maintained opportunity for socioeconomic self-improvement as a
major and essential feature. Young people may improve upon the
positions of their parents, or they may fall below the level of their
parents. They may be upward mobile or downward mobile.

In this chapter we shall ask how much mobility there is in the study
group thus far, and what conditions contribute to mobility. What
factors determine the socioeconomic status of River City youth as they
reach early adulthood? What is the relative importance of: family
social status, progress in school, intelligence, status in the adolescent
peer group?

The Measurement of Incipient Adult Status

Since members of the study group were only about 19 years old at
the time the study was closed, they did not have time to achieve their
final adult socioeconomic positions. This will take another 25 or 30
years. However, they already show an "incipient adult status" that
is probably a fairly good predictor of their final adult position. Accordingly, they were rated on incipient adult status on the following
scale. (If a girl is married, she is given the rating of her husband.

143

Otherwise, she is judged on education, job, and residence as if she were a boy, but her work experience is judged more leniently.)

Level A—Upper-middle or upper class
 Successful completion of first year of college and intention to continue.
 High-school graduate and successful work in a white-collar job, with evidence that promotion will come.
 Home situation good, from the point of view of space, location, and upkeep.

Level B—Lower-middle class
 If started in college, has dropped out or does not intend to return for second year.
 High-school graduate and a white-collar job which seems steady but does not promise much promotion.
 High-school graduate and apprenticed or getting trained for a highly skilled manual trade—electrician, photo-engraving, etc.
 A dropout from school will seldom make this level, but he may do so, if he has a white-collar job and is really making good in it.
 Home situation is good, but not quite so favorable as in Class A.
 Shows some evidence of interest in joining associations—lodge, church society, etc.

Level C—Upper-lower class
 High-school graduates not in A or B will probably belong here.
 The job should require some skill and some learning ability, and the person should have worked successfully at this job—often a skilled trade for which he is apprenticed.
 Most jobs at this level will be manual, though it includes simple white-collar jobs that have little chance for promotion.
 A boy who has been in the armed service and sent to a special training unit will probably belong here, or higher. A boy who has been in the service and has made a good job adjustment at a manual level on his return will belong here.
 The home situation should be tolerable, but below level B.

Level D—Lower-lower class
 Semiskilled or unskilled job without much promise of stability or good pay. Military service without any special training. No evidence of progress toward a career.
 Home is inadequate, physically and socially.

Two staff members rated the group separately and then discussed all cases of disagreement, arriving at agreement in this way.

This rating gives undue weight to successful completion of the first year of college, and thus swells the numbers in Class A unduly. Some of these people will end in lower-middle or B positions. Thus Class A is magnified at the expense of Class B.

There is another factor that will ultimately increase Class B. In time a number of high-school graduates who did not go to college,

TABLE 44. SOCIAL CLASS POSITION OF STUDY GROUP AS YOUNG ADULTS COMPARED WITH THE POSITION OF THEIR PARENTS

Incipient Adult Status of the Study Group

Parental Status	D	C	B	A	No info.	Total
A	0	2	7	30	4	43
B	6	38	29	38	17	128
C	34	73	37	19	23	186
D	53	38	5	2	30	128
No info.	0	0	0	0	2	2
Total	93	151	78	89	76	487

Type and Amount of Mobility

Parental Status	Upward Mobile	Stable	Downward Mobile	Total
A	0	30	9	39
B	38	29	44	111
C	56	73	34	163
D	45	53	0	98
Total	139	185	87	411
Per cent	34	45	21	

and a few high-school dropouts, who are now rated C, will succeed well enough to get B positions as white-collar workers, supervisors, and foremen.

Thus Class B is underestimated by this method, whereas Classes A and C are probably overestimated. This should be kept in mind when interpreting the findings on mobility as shown in Table 44. According to this table, 34 per cent of the group are upward mobile, 21 per cent are downward mobile, and 45 per cent are stable, or have the same social positions as their parents. There is a correlation coefficient of .61 between parental status and incipient adult status. While 95 per cent of upper-middle class children, and 60 per cent of lower-middles maintain a middle-class status, a third of the upper-lowers and 7 per cent of the lower-lower of Class D seem destined to move up into middle class.

The Sources of Upward Mobility

Educational progress is clearly the major method of achieving upward mobility, as can be seen in Table 45. This is true almost by

TABLE 45. INCIPIENT ADULT STATUS AS RELATED TO EDUCATIONAL CAREER

Highest Educational Level	Numbers of Youth at Various Status Levels			
	A	B	C	D
College success	82	5	0	0
College dropouts	1	12	5	0
Nursing school or Business college	0	13	2	0
High-school grad.	5	45	86	14
Dropout				
12th grade	1	2	14	7
10–11th grade	0	1	34	33
7–9th grade	0	0	8	36
Total	89	78	149	90

definition since educational status plays such a large part in the determination of incipient adult status.

Personal-social adjustment is also closely related to incipient adult status as is seen in Table 46. One half of those with upper-quartile scores for social leadership in the sixth grade were in the A-level of incipient adult status.

The three factors of intelligence, personal-social adjustment, and family social class are joined together in the incipient adult status. This is seen by a comparison of those who are upward mobile with those who are downward mobile.

The Upward versus the Downward Mobile

The 139 boys and girls who promise to be upward mobile have been closely involved in the mobility process, though probably both as mobile, with results showing in Table 47. The differences between the two groups are quite marked, and more so when it is remembered that three-fourths of the upward mobile are from lower-class homes, while three-fifths of the decliners are from middle-class homes. Thus

TABLE 46. INCIPIENT ADULT STATUS AND SOCIAL LEADERSHIP AT THE SIXTH GRADE

Quartile for Sixth Grade Social Leadership	Incipient Adult Status of the Study Group					
	D	C	B	A	No info.	Total
IV (high)	1	26	21	58	12	118
III	15	38	32	18	15	118
II	26	42	19	11	20	118
I	46	43	6	2	21	118
No info.	5	2	0	0	8	15
Total	93	151	78	89	76	487

TABLE 47. COMPARISON OF UPWARD WITH DOWNWARD MOBILE YOUTH (PERCENTAGES OF EACH GROUP)

Characteristic	Upward Mobile ($N = 139$)	Decliners ($N = 87$)
From middle-class homes	27	61
Boys	45	54
From homes broken by divorce or separation	15	11
Highly aggressive	4	17
Highly withdrawn	6	14
Moderate or major delinquency	4	19
Religion fairly important or important	52	30
Top Quartile—California Psychological Inventory	36	10
Top Quartile—6th grade IQ	40	16
Top Quartile—Rank in high school class	37	12
High-school graduate	88	54
Success in first year of college	43	0

both the upward and the downward-mobile youth are strikingly different from the majority of the social class group from which they come.

The element of personal-social adjustment seems to be especially closely involved in the mobility process, though probably both as cause and effect. Thus the highly withdrawn and highly aggressive children tend strongly toward a class position lower than that of their parents, while those with high social-leadership scores are strongly upward mobile. Of some 50 children rated as the top 10 per cent in aggressive maladjustment in the sixth and seventh grades, all but two are incipient lower-class adults.

On the Sentence Completion Test given in the tenth grade the upward-mobile youngsters did especially well on the Autonomy and Acceptance of Others tasks. On the California Test of Personality, given in the seventh grade, two-thirds of the lower-class youth who now have incipient middle-class status had above-average scores, as opposed to only one-fourth of those who were not upward mobile.

Early Marriage and Social Mobility

Early marriage is rare among upper-middle class youth. In the River City group none of the boys married early, and all 5 girls who married by 18 married men who will help them maintain their middle class positions.

Children of lower-middle class families are more likely to find social mobility or even maintenance of lower-middle status difficult if they marry early. Of the 8 lower-middle class boys who married only 1 went on to college, and he was forced to quit when a child arrived. None of the 20 lower-middle class girls who married by the fall of 1959 went on to college, nor have any of them married college men. Since higher education is the most usual means of gaining or maintaining a middle-class position, few if any of the lower-middle class children who married early will rise on the social ladder, and a number are decliners.

Fay.   Fay is a lower-middle class girl who married out of weakness and made a poor marriage. Neither of Fay's parents had been graduated from high school, but they were both hard-working, God-fearing people. Her father, a skilled craftsman, built a home in an upper-middle class area in order to give Fay and her brother an opportunity to go to school with children from the "best" families, but somehow neither Fay nor her parents ever really "belonged" in this neighborhood. While Fay's parents wanted her to "get ahead" and saw to it that she took piano and ballet lessons, they were never able to make friends in the neighborhood. They maintained their membership in a church in a lower-class area, and joined nothing else.

Fay was not chosen as a friend on sociometric tests. Both her classmates and teachers agreed that she was quite withdrawn but had occasional outbursts of temper.

Fay's intellectual ability as measured by sixth-grade intelligence tests was average, but she tested lower in high school. She did poorly on high school achievement tests, and when she left school her grade-point average was in the bottom 5 per cent of her class.

In the eleventh grade Fay left school to marry a man who had served nine years in the navy. She worked briefly at a soda fountain, but was discharged because she "frequently came late and had an unpleasant personality." At the time of their marriage, her husband left the navy. He has held three jobs in the past year, none an improvement over the last. They now have two children and are living with her parents.

Although it could be argued that Fay's parents were never solidly middle class, it is surely true that Fay did not fulfill their dreams. She lacked both the outstanding ability and the personality needed to make social mobility possible. Her marriage to an irresponsible man was just another step along the road she was already taking.

Early marriage by youth of lower-class status has a more varied relation to social mobility. Among the children from Class C families, one-fifth of the boys and over two-fifths of the girls had married by the autumn of 1959, when most were 18 or 19 years old. Of the 40 girls, 10 married men whose jobs or successful college work indicate that they will secure middle-class positions and thus make their wives upward mobile. Of the 18 Class C boys who were married, only 2 are likely to be upward mobile. One of them married a high school classmate at graduation time and enlisted in the Air Force, where he has advanced rapidly in an electronics job. An unwanted pregnancy forced the other boy to get married before he finished high school, but his wife, a daughter of a teacher in another community, is a talented girl who has encouraged his efforts to get an education. He is working in a clothing store to support his family while he attends college.

A number of Class D girls married stable working-class men and moved up to Class C, while four Class D youths who married early seem likely to move up to middle-class status. Henry is one of them. He did well in high school, and while still in school began to work at a supermarket. Henry's boss reports that he is responsible and has a pleasing personality. He has done so well that he has been promoted to assistant manager of the store.

Marriage played a major role in Barbara's mobility. After her graduation from high school she took a job in a ten-cent store. She had planned to go to business college, but could not afford it. At the store she met and fell in love with a store executive, a college-trained man ten years older than herself. She is now married and raising a family. Barbara says, "My husband has a good job; we have a nice apartment and a new car. I never thought I would have it so good." Since Barbara had only average ability and no financial backing, marriage was probably the only road to middle-class status available to her.

Two Cases of Upward Mobility

Both Betty and Bruce illustrate the importance of ability, achievement motivation, personal adjustment, and family backing in social mobility.

Betty. Betty is the oldest of six children. Neither of her parents went to high school. Her father has a small but stable income from repairing washing machines. When Betty was a high-school sophomore her mother told an interviewer, "I want Betty to have a nice personality; I don't care much about the A's. Right now, Betty doesn't think she's going to get married for a long time, but I wish she had a little more domestic interest. I know what she wants to do after high school; she wants four years of college, but I've seen too many girls who wanted big things and most of them wound up in a store or in an office, or got married at eighteen. She wants to be a teacher, but I personally don't think she'll get it. We told the children we would put them through high school. If she goes further than that, she'll have to do it largely on her own."

Betty's name appeared on both the leadership and intellectual talent lists. Her pleasing personality won the hearts of her teachers and gave her a place in a group of upper-middle class girls she met in junior high school. Although Betty never complained, her mother sensed that Betty wanted nicer clothes than they could afford. Her mother said, "One time Betty was invited to a farewell party for one of her friends at the Country Club, but she asked us not to pick her up there when the dance was over. Her brother said that she was embarrassed about having us drive up in our prewar Ford, and I guess he was right. I can't blame her though."

Betty was near the top of her class in high school and is now attending a well-known university with the help of three scholarships. Although Betty's parents cannot help her financially, their moral support combined with her ability and high motivation to reach her goals have made her upward mobile.

Bruce. Bruce's mother played a more active role in making his mobility possible. Bruce was an only child. His father, an alcoholic, died when he was three. His mother had not finished high school, but she had a strong interest in music and enjoyed reading. It was necessary for her to take a semiskilled factory job in order to support her son.

During his mother's working hours, Bruce stayed at a well-run public nursery, but his mother often took him on long walks and talked and read to him whenever she could. Bruce soon had a large vocabulary and an inquisitive mind. He expected the people in his world to be friendly and helpful. The teachers at the nursery school were very pleased with this well-mannered boy, and when he arrived at elementary school the teachers there found him to be a "teacher's dream."

Although his mother didn't have much extra money she took Bruce to music concerts whenever possible and found him to be quite interested. One day he came home from school and told his mother that a teacher had given him a music test and thought that he would make a good trumpet player. She said, "I didn't let on like it made much difference to me, but I was so thrilled about it that I ran down and got him a trumpet in a hurry. He was serious about it ever since he started. I didn't want to say too much before that, because you can't push a kid into things like that, but for me, what he's done with his music is a dream come true."

Bruce had good intellectual ability, and a likeable personality. Even in his lower-class elementary school his closest friends were those with intellectual interests, and when he reached junior high school he quickly made meaningful contact with upper-middle class children with interests similar to his. He was frequently elected to class offices and when he began dating he went with upper-middle class girls.

By the time Bruce reached the ninth grade, his occupational plans were made. He wanted to be a music teacher. He studied bassoon and piano as well as trumpet. Somehow his mother found money for expensive instruments and lessons, and found time to play the piano herself and to go with Bruce to concerts. Bruce began playing in the local symphony, began to give music lessons, and at the urging of his music teachers and older friends, he did well in all his school courses. His only complaint about his high-school teachers was that some of them were not demanding enough, that they graded too much on the basis of personality and did not criticize work specifically enough. His highest praise of a teacher was to say that "he could make seemingly small things interesting and important. He always demanded but you weren't negatively pressured. You wanted to do well."

Bruce held numerous positions of leadership in high school, worked after school giving music lessons, dated upper-middle class girls, and saved his money for college. Now in his sophomore year at college he has an exceptional academic record and is well thought of by his classmates and his professors. Very few children from poor families are able to make the progress that this boy made. The differences arise out of his early childhood experiences with his mother. While she has always been careful not to press the boy to be one thing or another, and thus has encouraged autonomy in her son, she has been interested in many things herself, has encouraged an equalitarian attitude toward people of all socioeconomic classes, has provided her son with stimulating experiences, and has been willing to sacrifice economically in order to make it possible for him to have benefits of concerts, lectures, books, and a college education. With this kind of a mother behind him, Bruce's personality was such that he found the world smiling at him and received a great deal of encouragement. The men music teachers took over the role of father with this boy, provided the models he needed, and helped him get the music students he needed to earn money, and the scholarship aid he needed to make college possible. Several older middle-class friends of his wrote back from college urging Bruce to do well in all his subjects. Thus they too played a part. Bruce intends to get his master's degree. Eventually he plans to get a doctorate. The casual observer might be surprised that Bruce would rise so far. But one who studies the record realizes that the initial pattern was set before he entered school, and although he came from a home with little money, it was the type of home which made social mobility almost easy. There are undoubtedly many other lower-class boys and girls who, given a mother like this and insightful teachers, could develop their abilities to the extent that this boy has.

Conclusions

From this study of social mobility during childhood and adolescence three major conclusions emerge. First, River City offers boys and girls a fair degree of opportunity to rise above the level of their parents on the socioeconomic scale, but at the same time it requires considerable effort for them to avoid falling below their parents' level,

A third of them promise to rise on the social scale, while a fifth show signs of falling in social status.

Second, educational achievement is the usual way to climb in the social structure, although a few girls succeed by marrying stable, higher-placed men.   But high-school graduation is not enough to account for much social mobility.   Young people generally have to secure more education than their parents in order merely to maintain the socioeconomic level of their parents.

Third, as has appeared time and time again in this study, a successful social adjustment in the peer group appears to be equally, if not more, important than intelligence as a means of doing well in school and making a good start in adult life.   This should not be interpreted to mean that conformity to the peer group and other-directedness are the marks of future success.   The definition we have used of personal-social adjustment and the measures we have used stress such qualities as autonomy, acceptance of others, leadership, and sense of personal worth.

12

ADULT COMPETENCE

THE GOAL THAT THE YOUTH of River City are seeking may be called "adult competence." They want to become successful workers, parents, husbands, wives, and homemakers. Success in these roles spells adult competence, as they see it.

Although the age of 19 or 20 is too early to tell with great assurance how well a young person is going to achieve adult competence, it is possible to make a judgment as to his initial competence, or his initial adult adjustment. This kind of judgment has been made by means of a rating scale that uses all the information available on educational progress, job success, marital success, and personal competence. This rating scale follows.

High—4-5
   Adequate social adjustment in college and grades of at least C—. A summer job is a plus value.
   Marriage to a stable spouse as is evidenced by his stable work record, lack of delinquency, plans for the future, financial independence of parents, etc.
   Stable in work history or moving to more responsible jobs.
Average—3
   Fairly stable work history.
   In college but low grades even though trying; adequate job adjustment if dropped out of college.
   Fairly stable marriage.

Some outside interests and contacts with others.

Has found some satisfaction in job, marriage, education, or social
life.

Low—1–2

Unstable marriage.

Current delinquency.

Instability on the job.

Poor mental health evidenced.

Irresponsible attitude toward marriage, laws, the community, etc.
Primarily interested in self.

Low morale.

In general, plus values are given for such evidence of independence
and stability as buying a house, financial independence from parents,
plans for further education and for vocational advancement. Negative
values are given for poor living conditions even after several years of
marriage, close dependence on parents, job instability of spouse.

All the young people of the group were rated by two staff members,
working independently and using all the data available concerning
the individual's last year or two since he left high school. The information on which the rating was based included interviews with employers and college counsellors, interviews with the subject and visits
to his home, newspaper reports, court records, etc. The two judges
agreed perfectly on 80 to 85 per cent of the cases. When they disagreed, they conferred and agreed upon a joint rating.*

Factors Related to Initial Adult Competence

There are three kinds of qualities that predict adult competence.
These are: intellectual ability, family social status, and social adjustment. Tables 48 and 49 show how initial adult competence is related
to intelligence as measured in the sixth and seventh grades, and to
family social status. It is clear that children with high family social
status and high intelligence have enormously favorable chances of
gaining a high rating on initial adult adjustment.

In addition to these tables, the coefficients of correlation between
initial adult adjustment and the measures of family social status, intel-

* In this study we have used three indices of adult adjustment, obviously interrelated but also somewhat different from each other. They are: initial adult adjustment, incipient adult status, and work adjustment. They have high inter-
correlations, as follows: IAA-IAS, .85; IAA-WA, .83; IAS-WA, .60.

ligence, and social adjustment at ages 11 to 15 show a substantial degree of relationship. These correlation coefficients with initial adult adjustment are .48, .48, .52, —.24, .58 for socioeconomic status, IQ, social leadership, aggressive maladjustment, and social adjustment as measured by the California Psychological Inventory, respectively.

TABLE 48. INITIAL ADULT ADJUSTMENT AND INTELLECTUAL ABILITY

| IQ Quartile | Initial Adult Adjustment Rating | | | | | |
	5	4	3	2	1	Total
Q IV (high)	34	33	24	10	2	103
Q III	14	28	36	12	4	94
Q II	5	10	44	24	9	92
Q I (low)	1	5	42	24	16	88
No info.	5	6	8	8	7	34
Total	59	82	154	78	38	411

TABLE 49. INITIAL ADULT ADJUSTMENT AND PARENTAL SOCIAL STATUS

| Social Class of Family | Initial Adult Adjustment Rating | | | | | |
	5	4	3	2	1	Total
A	17	15	6	1	0	39
B	24	32	37	15	3	111
C	16	32	68	34	13	163
D	2	3	43	28	22	98
Total	59	82	154	78	38	411

Thus the social adjustment factor seems to have about the same weight in predicting adult competence as do intelligence and family social class.

Scores on social leadership at the sixth grade are seen in Table 50 to be rather closely related to ratings on initial adult adjustment. The same relationship is shown in another way in Table 12-1 (Appendix). Here the upper 10 per cent of boys and girls in social leadership, aggressive and withdrawn maladjustment are separated and examined for their initial adult adjustment. A high score on social leadership was almost a guarantee of a high adult competence rating. High scores on aggressive or withdrawn maladjustment were a strong indication of low or at best average adult competence.

Educational progress as related to initial adult adjustment is reported in Table 12-2 (Appendix). This shows a relationship that was

TABLE 50. INITIAL ADULT ADJUSTMENT AND PERSONAL-SOCIAL ADJUSTMENT AT THE SIXTH GRADE

Quartile for Sixth Grade Social Leadership	Initial Adult Adjustment Rating					
	5 (high)	4	3	2	1	Total
IV (high)	39	34	24	8	1	106
III	11	29	45	14	4	103
II	7	14	47	19	11	98
I	2	5	35	35	20	97
No info.	0	0	3	2	2	7
Total	59	82	154	78	38	411

present by definition, since educational level was taken into account in the rating on initial adult adjustment.

The Competent versus the Incompetent

In order to see more clearly what makes for success and for failure in initial adult adjustment, we separated the 59 boys and girls judged to be most competent and the 38 judged to be least competent and compared the two groups systematically on a number of factors. The factors on which the comparisons are based may be grouped into two categories. One set, called "background factors" includes family social class, family living arrangements, intelligence, and church relationships. These are things with which the child is endowed by his family, with the possible exception of church relationships, which are partly a matter of family instigation and partly a matter of choice by the boy or girl. The other set, called "performance factors," includes personal adjustment, delinquency, and marriage. These are matters over which the individual exercises more determination and more responsibility than for the background factors.

It is clear from Tables 51A and 51B that most of the boys and girls who turn out well as young adults have favorable home situations and favorable personal characteristics as children, and that they create a favorable situation for themselves in adolescence.

TABLE 51A. COMPARISON OF HIGH AND LOW INITIAL ADULT ADJUSTMENT GROUPS (BACKGROUND FACTORS)

	Male		Female	
	High	Low	High	Low
Number in Group	20	23	39	15
Social Class of Parents				
A	6	0	11	0
B	10	2	14	1
C	3	9	13	4
D	1	12	1	10
Living Arrangements				
With both parents	16	10	33	5
With one parent	3	6	3	7
With parent and step-parent	1	6	2	3
With relatives, institution, and other	0	1	1	0
Church Relationship				
Important	13	3	20	1
Little importance	3	2	8	6
Unknown to clergy	3	18	5	8
No information	1	0	6	0
Intelligence				
Q IV (high)	11	2	23	0
Q III	4	3	10	1
Q II	3	5	0	4
Q I (low)	1	9	0	7
No information	1	4	6	3

Conclusions

It is a fair conclusion, but an oversimple one, that the children who are endowed with advantages make the most of them during adolescence and become the most competent young adults. The evidence for this proposition is clear and impressive in the statistical sense.

On the other hand, the exceptions to this general proposition are important. The single Class D boy and the single Class D girl who appear in the group with the best adjustment are significant people.

They prove that there is a chance for children with disadvantages to
make good in River City.   Twenty per cent of the boys with the highest initial adult adjustment were below average in personal-social adjustment in school.

TABLE 51B. COMPARISON OF HIGH AND LOW INITIAL
ADULT ADJUSTMENT GROUPS (PERFORMANCE FACTORS)

	Male		Female	
	High	Low	High	Low
Number in Group	20	23	39	15
Aggressive Maladjustment (Grades 6, 7)				
Q IV (high)	3	11	5	3
Q III	1	3	4	3
Q II	4	1	10	2
Q I (low)	8	2	16	2
No information	4	6	4	5
Personal Adjustment (10th grade CPI)				
Q IV (high)	9	0	14	0
Q III	3	1	10	1
Q II	4	0	7	0
Q I (low)	1	4	0	3
No information	3	18	8	11
Delinquency				
Major I	0	10	0	1
II	0	2	0	0
III	0	4	0	1
Minor IV	1	4	0	4
Not delinquent	18	3	38	8
No information	1	0	1	1
Marriage—October 1959				
Not yet	19	13	33	3
Age 19+	0	6	2	0
18	1	0	3	3
17	0	1	0	2
16	0	3	1	3
Before 16	0	0	0	3
No information	0	0	0	1

At the same time, some boys and girls who had the advantages of
homes with high social status or who had good intelligence have failed
to achieve this early promise.   Two in the top quartile of intelligence
and four more in the third quartile had the lowest ratings for initial
adult adjustment.

Thus the achievement of adult competence is not an automatic matter emerging mechanically from a combination of favorable situations and personal qualities. It depends upon the efforts of boys and girls and of their families, aided or encumbered, as the case may be, by the circumstances of life.

Adjustment Groups. When the information on this group of boys and girls is assembled for a final survey, there appear six describable groups of young people. These may be called Adjustment Groups, each with its characteristic pattern of growing up.

TABLE 52. SOCIAL COMPOSITION AND MOBILITY PAT-
TERNS OF THE SEVERAL ADJUSTMENT GROUPS

Adjustment Group	Social Class of Origin (Percentages)				Total	Mobility Pattern
	A	B	C	D		
I	1	2	2	0	5	upward
II	6	14	0	0	20	upward & stable
III	0	0	11	3	14	upward
IV	2	10	4	0	16	downward
V	0	0	17	15	32	stable
VI	0	1	4	8	13	downward & stable
Total	9	27	38	26	100	

1. The able, creative persons, who have led rich lives themselves and will enrich the lives of their fellow-citizens. Possibly 5 per cent of boys and girls fall into this category, or about 20 persons in the River City cohort. They have emerged from a hundred who showed signs of talent as children. They have cultivated their talents by hard work and they have been stimulated and supported by family, community, and school.

2. Those who have had the advantages of above-average family status and have met the community expectations well. They have gone to college in most cases, though some of the girls have not done so. They are starting adulthood with every promise of becoming strong and capable maintainers of a productive society. As can be seen in Table 52, they make up about 20 per cent of the total group. They will all be middle-class people as adults, some of them mobile into upper-middle class.

3. Those without the advantages of middle-class families, who have nevertheless done as well as the middle-class children. They have succeeded in school, most of them are in college, and they will all be upward mobile into middle-class adult positions. The school and community have given these 14 per cent unusually good treatment, and the young people have responded with economic and social competence.

4. The drifters, who perform indifferently under the prodding of family and school. Coming from the middle classes and the upper-working class, these 16 per cent are the underachievers of life, performing less well than their parents and teachers expect. They constitute the main body of downward mobility.

5. The largest group of all, who maintain the working-class positions of their fathers and are content to do so. None of them goes to college, and many of them drop out of high school, but they make a stable adjustment to working-class life. Amounting to 32 per cent in the River City cohort, they will be the typical working men of the next generation.

6. The alienated ones, who have experienced neglect at home and failure in school; these are the core of the lower-lower class of the next generation. They see nothing to gain by hard work or study, and will contribute little except trouble to their adult generation. These, 13 per cent, represent the main source of social pathology in River City.

By the time they are 11 or 12 years old, the boys and girls of River City give pretty clear evidence to an observing eye of the Adjustment Group into which they will fit. By combining data on their school achievement, personal-social adjustment, and family social class, it is possible to predict with considerable accuracy what kind of adult adjustment they are headed for.

13

MAKING A JUDGMENT

HOW WELL DO THE YOUTH of River City accomplish the tasks of growing up to become competent workers, parents, husbands and wives, and community members? The answer to this question cannot be very deep at a time when the generation being studied is only 19 or 20 years old. For instance, it cannot deal with the question of how well these young people are prepared to meet the tests of citizenship in a time of world interdependence and threatened nuclear destruction. It must remain on the level of the immediate concerns of the young people themselves, which have to do with making a living and raising a family and getting started as newcomers in the world of adults.

How well has River City done in providing boys and girls with the means of growing up? To what extent has the community equalized the life chances of the youth born into families of lower status with those born into middle-class families? To what extent has the community provided opportunity for youth with *various* kinds of abilities to develop those abilities in constructive fashion? Or has the community encouraged and assisted only the group with intellectual ability?

What should River City do, in order to make itself a better place for boys and girls?

Cooperation of Social Classes

In a complex society the various social groups must live in harmony with one another and must cooperate in many things in order to make

162

the community a good place to live.   The various social classes must each perform their functions in making the community run smoothly.

Yet there is a good deal of conflict between social classes, as other community studies have shown; and some of this is reflected in the attitudes of boys and girls in school toward others of different social class, as has been illustrated in some of the interviews reported here.

The public schools inevitably reflect hostilities between classes if such hostilities exist; but a good school system teaches boys and girls of different social backgrounds to get along together, and thus build a cohesive society.

A good school system builds toward a cohesive society by preparing boys and girls to find places satisfactory to them in the adult society. This means that the school system prepares the majority of boys and girls to follow pretty much in the footsteps of their parents, but also that a sizable and important minority of lower-class boys and girls are prepared for life in a higher social class than the one they were born into.

A review of the facts about the Adjustment Groups described in Chapter 12 will help us to assess the degree of success River City has had through its school system and other community institutions in building a cohesive society.

Groups 1 and 3 are the upward-mobile ones, making up 19 per cent of the age group.   They are the ones whose life chances have been enhanced by the schools and other youth-serving agencies.   They are the ones to whom River City can point with pride as products of a democratic society that extends opportunity to able youth.

Groups 2 and 5 are the stable ones, who will lead satisfying and constructive lives at the same social class levels as their parents, either middle class or working class.   They make up 52 per cent of the age group.   Although the schools might have done a better job with them through stimulating them to more intellectual effort and more artistic activity, they are, nevertheless, the great stabilizing force of the next generation.

Groups 4 and 6 are those with whom River City has failed, and there are a dangerous 29 per cent of them.   The drifters and the alienated, they have not made use of what the schools offered them, and the community has not been able to offset what in many cases was an inadequate home and in some probably an inferior biological constitution.   They come from all social classes in roughly equivalent proportions, though the lower-middle class seems to furnish more than its proportional share of them.   They are the elements making for instability and disunity in the society.

Opportunity for Growth

The schools and the other youth-serving and youth-orienting agencies described in Chapter 1 do two essential things. First, they provide avenues of growth toward adulthood. Second, they increase the life chances of boys and girls from disadvantaged homes.

Opportunities for the Disadvantaged. There are several types of disadvantage that may hamper a child. Foremost, in our judgment, is the disadvantage of low socioeconomic status, and especially of the lowest, or D-class status. Others are inferior family life, physical disability, and mental inferiority. We have not described the attempts of River City to increase the opportunities of the physically and mentally inferior, beyond noting that there are special classes for these boys and girls, and that the school system spends more money per pupil on them than on the average pupils. The disadvantages that go with low social status are illustrated in the figure entitled "Social Class and Facts About Youth in River City." Here the data from several of the tables previously shown have been combined into a set of "index scores" which show how the children of various social classes fare with respect to some favorable and some unfavorable elements in their lives. The general tendency is clearly in favor of children from homes of higher socioeconomic status, in spite of the fact that a substantial number of lower-class children do quite well in life.

We have seen that with respect to the handicap of low socioeconomic status the youth-serving institutions do a great deal to help these boys and girls who "fit in" to the prevailing system of values and of opportunities in schools, churches, and youth organizations. Adjustment Group 3, with 14 per cent of the youth in it, shows that much can be accomplished and much has been accomplished to increase the life chances of such boys and girls.

However, the schools and other youth-serving organizations have not been able to make up for the disadvantages to which Adjustment Groups 4 and 6 are subject—disadvantages not only of a socioeconomic nature but also of inadequate homes, and of physique and mind. About 30 per cent of the age group are unmotivated for school work, to say the least. In addition, at least half of this group are alienated from the values of the community and of the school. They have no feeling of belonging to community or school, and they do not expect anything good from these institutions.

A System of Differential Opportunities. River City tends to offer opportunity to disadvantaged youth on the community's own terms, as it were. The community seems to be saying, "Boys and girls, we can offer grand opportunities for those of you who can do well in school, and will attend school regularly, and take part in church activities, and join the Scouts or the 'Y'." But to youngsters without these qualities the community has little to offer. Jobs are scarce for youth. Early marriage is frowned on. Boys and girls with unusual abilities (except for musical abilities) do not get much encouragement.

Perhaps River City needs a system of differential opportunities for youth with various kinds of ability and interest, including those who already are getting along pretty well. The churches, for example, might offer opportunities for social leadership as well as for moral development to youth who do not fit readily into the social patterns of the high school. There is some evidence that the churches are doing this for some boys and girls.

The Society for Fine Arts and the Little Theater are beginning to offer opportunities for boys and girls with artistic and dramatic abilities.

The more avenues for development in the community, the greater is the probability that every person will develop competence in some constructive direction.

Above all, there is need for alternative opportunities for boys and girls who do poorly in school. This need has emerged clearly in the chapters dealing with delinquency, with early marriage, and with work. It is the boys and girls of this group who make up the large part of the alienated and the indifferent adjustment groups.

Just as the schools and the churches and the Little Symphony offer stimulation and avenues of development for youth with certain types of ability, institutions are needed for youth with other potentialities, even though these others may not be so valuable in the eyes of the community.

Work Experience. In the chapter on work it was pointed out that for the youth who do poorly in school, there is need of an alternative pathway to adulthood through work experience. Since the American economy has fewer and fewer jobs for juveniles, perhaps the school should provide a program of supervised work experience leading to an adult job. This experience might well start as early as age 13, in the seventh or eighth grade, as part of a work-study program. It should involve experience and training in the simplest kinds of useful work for boys and girls, such as keeping parks and playgrounds in order, safety patrol, care of young children in a day nursery.

The first phase of the program would consist of learning such simple habits and attitudes as punctuality, cooperation in a work group, respect for the role of foreman or boss, rather than more complex work skills.   The boys and girls in this program are the ones who need the elemental habits and attitudes most, as can be seen from the work-adjustment ratings on the River City school dropouts.

After they have progressed through this first stage of learning basic work habits and attitudes, youngsters in the work-study program should move on to individual part-time jobs during school hours, in which the employer and the school work-supervisor work together to make this an educational experience for the boy or girl.   This might begin at the age of 14 to 16.

On the basis of two or three years of improving work adjustment in this phase of the work-study program, the youth would be ready, at the age of 16 or 17, to take a full-time job with a good prospect for growth into maturity.   Alternatively, the youth at this age might be ready for vocational training in high school to prepare him for a trade.

According to the experience of the River City study group, as many as 20 per cent of an age group might profit substantially from such a work-study program, and at least 10 per cent, mainly boys, might be saved from severe maladjustment and delinquency.

Such a program would require a major effort and a major reorientation on the part both of school teachers and of employers in River City, who, as in most communities, do not see this sort of thing as their responsibility.

Preparing Girls for Early Marriage.   The other principal avenue of growth is marriage, and Chapter 9 has shown that this is chosen by many girls who are not succeeding well in school.   Possibly the school could develop a program for girls leading to a more successful marriage that would be the counterpart of a work-study program for boys.

Commencing at about the eighth grade, the girls who are obviously headed for early dropping out of school might be assigned to a woman teacher who is a combination of social worker and home economics teacher.   This teacher would expect to work with this group of girls for the next four or five years, whether they stayed in school or not.

The school work of these girls would be organized around their needs as wives and mothers soon-to-be.   They would do work in homemaking, child care, clothing, and personal grooming.   They would have a modified program in English, science and social studies under other teachers.   They would be encouraged to get jobs as baby-sitters, and might be excused from school half of the day to work in homes, their own or those of other people, taking care of children and doing housework. This part-time work arrangement might come after they reached the age of 15, and would be supervised by the teacher.

The teacher would organize these girls into a social club, with parties and dances, and with incidental teaching in the social skills of dancing, entertaining, etc. The teacher would try to assume the roles of friend, confidante, club-leader, and big sister to the girls. She would encourage them to come to her for counsel on such matters as choice of a boy friend, what to do about petting, whether to marry, and so forth.

When the girls neared the age of 16, the meetings of the group would include club meetings at convenient times for those who had quit school, at convenient and acceptable places such as settlement houses, YWCA, Salvation Army, churches, in case the girls did not wish to meet in school buildings.

As the girls grew older, they would have dances, parties to announce their engagements, "showers" for those about to be married and for those expecting babies. The group would give its members a source of emotional support when needed, would help those who were having difficulty with their marriages, and would set up expectations of behavior for girls as teen-agers and young wives and mothers that would reduce the dangers of sexual promiscuity on the one hand, and social isolation on the other.

The teacher or club leader might carry two groups of girls at a given time, a younger group of girls aged 13 to 16, who were in school and under her direct supervision, though they would have other teachers for some of their studies; and an older group aged 16 to 18 or 19, many of whom out of school, and whom she would see at evening or afternoon club meetings, and in individual conferences.

Some such school program as this may offer the school its last chance of serving this important and neglected group of girls.

These examples illustrate the general principle that the community of River City and many other communities can do a better job, through their schools and other youth-serving agencies, of providing avenues of satisfactory growth for all kinds of boys and girls, academic and nonacademic.

APPENDIX

RIVER CITY PUBLICATIONS

The following publications are referred to frequently in the text. They give many technical details that could not be reported here for lack of space.

1. Bowman, Paul H., et al., "Studying Children and Training Counselors in a Community Program." *Supplementary Educational Monographs,* No. 78. University of Chicago Press, 1953.
2. Bowman, Paul H., and Charles V. Matthews, *Motivations of Youth for Leaving School.* Cooperative Research Project No. 200. U.S. Office of Education and Youth Development Project, Committee on Human Development, University of Chicago, 1960.
3. Liddle, Gordon, "Overlap Among Desirable and Undesirable Characteristics in Gifted Children." *Journal of Educational Psychology,* 49: 219–223, 1958.
4. Pierce, James V. and P. H. Bowman, *The Educational Motivation Patterns of Superior Students Who Do and Do Not Achieve in High School.* Cooperative Project No. 208. U.S. Office of Education. Cooperative Research Monograph No. 2. U.S. Printing Office, Washington, 1960.
5. Pierce, James V., *Sex Differences in Achievement Motivation.* Cooperative Project No. 1097. U.S. Office of Education. U.S. Printing Office, Washington, 1961.
6. Stivers, Eugene, "Motivation for College in High School Boys," *School Review,* 66: 341–350 (1958).
7. Stivers, Eugene, "Motivation for College in High School Girls." *School Review,* 67: 320–334 (1959).

NOTE ON STATISTICAL SIGNIFICANCE

The usual statistical tests have been computed whenever reference is made to a statistical inference. Generally the chi-square technique has been used, and occasionally a t-test for significance of the difference between means. The significance level is usually stated. Where this has not been done, and a finding has been reported as reliable, this means that the finding was significant at the 5 per cent level or beyond.

THE SOCIAL STRUCTURE OF RIVER CITY

The socioeconomic status of each child in the study group was determined by means of the Index of Status Characteristics (ISC), a score based on four facts concerning the family of the child.   These four facts are:*

Occupation of the father, rated according to the rating scale developed by Warner.

House-type, rated according to size and condition of the house and grounds.

Area-type, a rating of the dwelling area according to River City standards of prestige.   The dwelling areas of River City are shown in a simplified schematic map in Figure 2.

Source of Income of the family, rated on a scale of prestige from a high for "inherited income" to a low for living on public charity.

The ISC ranges from 12 to 84, and is used for studies where a socioeconomic score is needed.   But in this book the concept of social class will also be used, which requires us to identify a social class by means of ISC scores.

The procedure for defining the boundaries of social classes was to study sample cases whose ISC's lay close on either side of the dividing line established in earlier community studies.   The dividing line for River City was determined in such a way as to make the majority of borderline cases fall into the classes they fit best.   In this way the following points were established.

Upper and Upper-Middle Class, Group A	39 and less
Lower-Middle Class, Group B	40–55
Upper-Lower Class, Group C	56–67
Lower-Lower Class, Group D	68–84

Effects of Omission of the Catholic Parochial School Children

In chapter 1 it was noted that some 32 per cent of elementary school children in River City were in Roman Catholic parochial schools, and were omitted from the study.   This means that perhaps 200 children of the age of our study group were not included in the early years of the study.   Almost 50 of them entered the public high school in the ninth grade, and were included from that time on.

* For more detail on the socioeconomic data concerning River City, see Paul H. Bowman, et al. "Studying Children and Training Counselors in a Community Program," Chapter 7.   For the technical details of the study of social stratification see the following books: W. Lloyd Warner, Marchia L. Meeker, and Kenneth W. Eells, *Social Class in America.*   New York: Harper Torchbooks, 1960.   August B. Hollingshead, *Elmtown's Youth.*   New York: John Wiley and Sons, 1949.

Those who were not included in the study were nearly all Roman Catholics, though a substantial number of children of Roman Catholic families were also in the study in the elementary and secondary school grades. The addition of the parochial school children would have had the following effects: the proportions of Class B and Class C children would have been increased somewhat, at the expense of Class A and Class D numbers. We do not have any substantial basis for estimating the change in the numbers of delinquent youth, or of youth entering college, although we suppose that the *proportions* of youth in these categories would not have changed appreciably. However, we believe that the *proportions* of youth known to a church would have been increased, and the *proportions* of very early marriages would have decreased. We have no basis for predicting anything about the effect of inclusion of data on parochial school children on the sizes of the correlation coefficients reported in the study.

THE MEASUREMENT OF INTELLIGENCE

For the measurement of intelligence a number of quite different group tests were used with the sixth graders, so as to avoid the tendency of a single test to select children with a specific type of mental ability. The following tests were used:

The SRA Primary Mental Abilities Test, given by the schools in the fourth grade.

The Goodenough Draw-a-Man Test. This test is not good for use with children beyond the sixth grade, but it seemed to work well with this group, except that its maximum IQ was 140, and therefore it penalized a few of the abler children.

The Davis-Eells Games, Elementary Form A, 1952. This was a nonverbal test, as was the Draw-a-Man, and was intended to be fairer to working-class children than the verbal tests were.

The Chicago Tests of Primary Mental Ability, Intermediate Form. This was chosen to allow the abler children to show their superiority in this test that was designed for ages 11–17. Three of the subtests were used—Vocabulary, Space, and Reasoning.

The Thurstone Concealed Figures Test, Form A, 1950. This was chosen because it tests Thurstone's second Closure factor, and was believed by Thurstone to be somewhat related to creativity.

All the tests except the SRA Primary Mental Abilities Test, which had been given in the fourth grade, were administered under the supervision of the research staff and scored by them. Scores were corrected for age differences among the pupils, if necessary, and eventually were combined to give an average IQ. The method of combining the several test scores is described in the monograph by Bowman et al. (1953).

The children in the Educable Mentally Handicapped group did not take the group tests. There was an individual Binet or Wechsler test IQ on each of them, and these were used.

Pupils entering after the sixth grade were given several of the tests when they were in the eighth or ninth grades.

THE MEASUREMENT OF PERSONAL AND SOCIAL ADJUSTMENT

The principal measures of adjustment were the *Behavior Description Chart* and the Who Are They? test. These instruments were developed over a period of three years, and were based on earlier work done by Hewitt and Jenkins, Sisson, and Ullmann.*

The Behavior Description Chart and the Who Are They? test as used in the ninth grade, are reproduced here. They are revisions of the forms used in the sixth and seventh grades. The Behavior Description Chart, which originally consisted of eighteen pentads, was reduced to ten pentads on the basis of item analysis. The Who are They? test originally included nineteen items. These were given factor analysis,† and three factors were extracted.

One was clearly a leadership or social effectiveness factor, made up of leadership and friendship items. The other two factors were ob-

* Lester Eugene Hewitt and Richard L. Jenkins, M.D. *Fundamental Patterns of Maladjustment.* Springfield, Illinois: State of Illinois, 1946. E. Donald Sisson. "Forced Choice: The New Army Rating," *Personnel Psychology* I (1948), 365–81. Charles A. Ullmann. *The Identification of Maladjusted School Children.* Public Health Monograph No. 1. Public Health Service Publication No. 211. Washington, D.C.: Government Printing Office, 1952.

For a full description of the techniques used, see Paul H. Bowman et al, *Mobilizing Community Resources for Youth. Supplementary Educational Monograph* No. 85. Chicago: University of Chicago Press, 1956. See also, Paul H. Bowman, et al, "Studying Children and Training Counselors in a Community Program." *Supplementary Educational Monograph* No. 78. Chicago: University of Chicago Press, 1953.

† James V. Mitchell, Jr. "The Factor Analysis of a 'Guess-Who' Questionnaire Designed to Identify Significant Behavior Patterns in Children." *Journal of Personality.* 24 June, (1956) 376–386.

viously maladjustment factors but were not so clearly differentiated from each other. This indicated that aggressive and withdrawn maladjustment were not sharply distinguished from one another, but it seemed desirable to retain them as separate variables.

The distribution of scores on these instruments is not normal. The scores cluster at the high-score end, with 7 to 10 per cent of the children receiving half of all the nominations on the WAT, and the remainder spread over the scale with another cluster receiving a score of zero or only one or two nominations. This means that the children who rank high are clearly identified, whereas the relative positions of the low-ranking children can shift a good deal from one test to another with a change of only one or two in their scores. Thus these instruments are fairly good for the identification of the out-

TABLE 3-1. RELATIONS OF 6TH-7TH GRADE ADJUSTMENT SCORES TO 9TH GRADE SCORES, BDC AND WAT COMBINED (PRODUCT-MOMENT CORRELATION COEFFICIENTS)

	N	Leadership	Aggression	Withdrawal
Boys	153	.45	.56	.51
Girls	156	.72	.50	.53

standing children, but not very good for measuring the positions of the remainder. For this reason, among others, a good deal of use was made of lists of the top 10 per cent of children in the three adjustment variables.

The statistical reliability of these instruments is not very high, by reason of the scoring characteristics just cited. A test of reliability was run between the scores of children in the sixth grade and in the seventh grade. This was a severe reliability check as a year elapsed between testings, and the children were in different classrooms, with 25 to 60 per cent turnover in class membership, and different teachers. The test-retest coefficients of correlation varied from .40 to .74 on the two instruments, being higher for social-leadership scores than for maladjustment scores.

Combining the BDC and WAT rankings gave greater stability to a child's scores, and the scores from sixth and seventh-grade testing were also combined to give even greater reliability. When the sixth and seventh-grade combined scores were compared with scores from similar testing in the ninth grade, the product-moment correlation coefficients are shown in Table 3-1.

The California Psychological Inventory developed by Gough* was employed with some modification to make it more readily usable by high school students. In effect, this meant the use of 359 out of 480 items from the Inventory as generally used, and 12 of the 18 original categories.

The Sentence Completion Test was developed by Gordon Liddle† and is probably a good projective instrument for measurement of personal-social adjustment in high-school age youth. Its reliability has been proved, but it has not been validated against a criterion of personal adjustment.

THE "WHO ARE THEY?" TEST (REVISED)

Here are some descriptions of different kinds of boys and girls. Read each description and ask yourself: "Which boys and girls in our group are like this?" Look over the list of names of your group to find the ones that fit each description. *Under* each question write the names of as many boys and girls as you think fit the description. Do *not* write your own name under any of the questions.

1. Who are the boys and girls who make good plans?
2. Who are the good leaders? They are leaders in several things.
3. Who are the boys and girls who stay out of games? They don't like to play hard.
4. Who are the ones who break rules—rules of the school and rules of games?
5. Who are the ones who seem to understand things most easily, out of school and in school?
6. Who are the boys and girls who always work for the good of their class, or their team, or their playmates?
7. Who are the ones who are too shy to make friends easily? It is hard to get to know them.
8. Who are the ones who complain about things? Nothing makes them happy. They want to have their own way.
9. Who are the ones who get bothered and upset when they are called on to talk or recite? They cannot tell as much as they really know.
10. Who are the most popular boys and girls?
11. Who are the ones who are timid and afraid to take chances?

* Harrison G. Gough. *The California Psychological Inventory.* Palo Alto, California: Consulting Psychologists Press, Inc. Gordon S. Liddle, "The California Psychological Inventory and Certain Social and Personal Factors." *Journal of Educational Psychology,* 49 (1958), 144–149.

† Gordon S. Liddle, "A Study of the Relationships of Talent, Maladjustment, Sex, and Social Status to Maturity in Adolescents." Unpublished Ph.D. Dissertation. Library of the University of Chicago, 1959.

12. Which boys and girls quarrel and get mad easily?
13. Who are the ones who are sure to have ideas for games and other interesting things to do, both out of school and in school?
14. Who are the ones who are mean and cruel to other children?
15. Who are the boys and girls you would like for your best friends?

THE BEHAVIOR DESCRIPTION CHART (REVISED)

Directions: In *each* of the sets of descriptive statements below, pick out two statements. (1) Pick out that statement which you find fits the child most aptly—the one which the child is *most like*. (2) Then pick out the statement which the child is *least like*. Place the letters of these statements on the record sheet under the number corresponding to the set of statements. Do not be concerned if the statement does not apply exactly, and do not dwell too long upon your decision. Go through the entire chart for one child at a time. Experience shows that the ratings can be completed in just a few minutes per child.

1. A. Others come to him for help
    B. Causes disturbances
    C. Lacks confidence in himself
    D. Reports those who break the rules
    E. Shows emotions in a restrained way

2. A. Other children find it hard to get along with him
    B. Is easily confused
    C. Other children are eager to be near him or on his side
    D. Likes to see things done his way
    E. Interested in other people's opinions and activities

3. A. Sensitive, touchy, hurt by criticism
    B. Shows off, attention-getter
    C. Is self-confident
    D. Enjoys being a part of the group without taking the lead
    E. Dislikes criticism

4. A. Is extremely quiet and passive
    B. Is a natural leader
    C. Is boastful
    D. Does his share but does not seek leadership
    E. Is generous when in the mood

5. A. Frequently gets into fights
    B. Helps to make and enforce rules
    C. Seems anxious and fearful
    D. Criticizes other people
    E. Is generous when in the mood

6. A. Makes sensible, practical plans
   B. Breaks rules
   C. Becomes discouraged easily
   D. Usually willing to share with others
   E. Does not care what others think

7. A. Takes an active part in group projects and other activities
   B. Is shy and retiring
   C. Others cannot work with him
   D. Polite
   E. Assertive

8. A. Quarrelsome
   B. Is tense or ill at ease when reciting or appearing before a group
   C. Likes jobs which give him responsibility
   D. Is quiet and seems content with himself
   E. Enjoys a conversation

9. A. His presence or absence is not noticed by other children
   B. Figures out things for himself
   C. Is impulsive and easily excited
   D. Is a good follower
   E. Is usually courteous to other children

10. A. Tries to bully and domineer over others
    B. Is quick to see valuable things in other people's suggestions
    C. Is hard to know
    D. Is boisterous
    E. Pleasant to talk with but seldom initiates a conversation.

TABLE 4-1. COMPARISONS OF ACHIEVERS WITH NON-ACHIEVERS AMONG HIGH ABILITY TWELFTH GRADE STUDENTS

	Achievers		Non-achievers		Level of Significance
	Mean	S.D.	Mean	S.D.	
Strength of educational motivation scores					
Boys	22.5	4.93	19.00	6.27	.05
Girls	22.0	5.34	16.88	6.18	.01
Socioeconomic status					
Boys	55.52	5.63	52.75	5.73	n.s.
Girls	56.00	5.84	53.46	6.95	n.s.
n-Achievement scores					
Boys	3.75	1.89	2.92	3.46	n.s.
Girls	6.12	4.68	4.96	4.66	n.s.

Note: there are 24 boys in each of the two groups, and there are 26 girls in each group.

TABLE 4-2. COMPARISON OF ACHIEVERS AND NON-ACHIEVERS ON MEASURES OF PERSONAL-SOCIAL ADJUSTMENT

	Achievers		Non-Achievers		
	Mean	S.D.	Mean	S.D.	P-value
California Psychological Inventory Scores					
Subjects					
Boys ($N = 25$)	56.6	6.1	49.6	7.5	.001
Girls ($N = 26$)	56.0	4.8	54.4	5.2	n.s.
Who Are They? Scores					
Aggression					
Boys ($N = 24$)	44.7	7.0	51.0	8.8	.05
Girls ($N = 26$)	45.4	6.5	44.9	6.4	n.s.
Withdrawal					
Boys	46.4	9.5	45.8	7.6	n.s.
Girls	43.6	8.0	47.7	10.7	.10
Leadership					
Boys	58.9	8.2	52.8	10.7	.01
Girls	62.2	7.4	57.1	11.0	.05
Behavior Description Chart Scores					
Aggression					
Boys	47.3	7.6	49.9	8.3	.13
Girls	45.9	6.7	46.4	8.9	n.s.
Withdrawal					
Boys	45.1	10.8	43.2	8.8	n.s.
Girls	43.9	11.2	47.5	8.9	.15
Leadership					
Boys	57.6	9.5	52.9	8.5	.05
Girls	61.7	7.5	56.2	7.3	.02

Note: The scores are *T*-scores. The *N*'s are the numbers of boys and girls in each of the Achiever and Nonachiever groups.

TABLE 5-1. SCHOOL HISTORY OF A COHORT OF RIVER CITY YOUTH (PERCENTAGES OF EACH SEX GROUP)

Social Class

Quartile for IQ	Highest Level	Male					Female				
		A	B	C	D	Total	A	B	C	D	Total
IV	College	3.5	6.0	3.0	0.5	13.0	4.5	5.5	4.5	0	14.5
	H.S. grad	0	1.0	3.0	2.5	6.5	1.0	6.0	4.0	0.5	11.5
	H.S. dropout	0	0.5	1.0	0.5	2.0	0	1.0	0	0.5	1.5
III	College	2.5	3.5	2.5	0	8.5	2.0	2.5	3.5	0	8.0
	H.S. grad	1.0	3.5	2.5	1.0	8.0	0	2.0	6.0	2.5	10.5
	H.S. dropout	0.5	0.5	6.5	2.0	9.5	0	2.0	2.0	2.0	6.5
II	College	0.5	1.0	1.5	0	3.0	0	1.0	0	0	1.0
	H.S. grad	1.0	3.5	4.0	4.0	12.5	0	3.0	6.0	3.0	12.0
	H.S. dropout	0	2.5	3.0	7.0	12.5	0.5	0.5	6.0	7.0	14.0

I	College	0	1.0	0	0.5	1.5	1.5	0	0.5	0	2.0
	H.S. grad	0	2.5	2.5	1.5	6.0	0.5	1.5	5.0	0	7.0
	H.S. dropout	0	8.5	8.5	9.0	18.0	0	1.5	3.5	7.0	12.0
Total	College	6.5	11.5	7.0	1.0	26.0	8.0	9.0	8.5	0	25.0
	H.S. grad	2.0	10.5	12.0	9.0	33.0	1.5	12.5	21.0	6.0	41.0
	H.S. dropout	0.5	4.5	19.0	18.0	42.0	0.5	5.0	11.5	17.0	34.0
	Grand total	9.0	26.5	37.5	27.0	100	10.0	26.5	40.5	23.0	100
	Number of persons	18	54	77	56	205	20	54	84	46	204

Note: Percentages are rounded to the nearest 0.5 per cent, and consequently the sums may not total exactly 100 per cent. This table is based on information concerning 409 boys and girls, and therefore does not agree completely with Table 14, in Chapter 5. The term "college" for highest educational level includes those who went to noncollegiate post-high school institutions.

TABLE 5-2. SOCIAL CLASS AND INTELLIGENCE OF HIGH SCHOOL DROP-OUTS (PERCENTAGES OF THE TOTAL COHORT, BY SEX)

Quartile for IQ	Age at Dropout	Male					Female				
		A	B	C	D	Total	A	B	C	D	Total
IV	Less than 16	0	0	0	0	0	0	0	0	0	0
	16 to 16.5	0	0	0.5	0.5	1.0	0	0	0	0.5	0.5
	Over 16.5	0	0.5	0.5	0	1.0	0	1.0	0	0	1.0
III	Less than 16	0	0	0	1.0	1.0	0	0	0.5	0.5	1.0
	16 to 16.5	0	0	1.0	0.5	1.5	0	0.5	1.0	0.5	2.0
	Over 16.5	0.5	0.5	5.5	0.5	7.0	0	1.5	0.5	1.5	3.5
II	Less than 16	0	0	0.5	1.0	1.5	0	0	1.5	2.0	3.5
	16 to 16.5	0	1.0	0.5	2.5	4.0	0	0	0.5	3.5	4.0
	Over 16.5	0	1.5	2.0	3.5	7.0	0.5	0.5	4.0	1.5	6.5

Social Class

I	Less than 16	0	0.5	1.0	1.0	2.5	0	0.5	1.0	1.0	2.5
	16 to 16.5	0	0.5	2.0	3.5	6.0	0	1.0	0.5	5.0	6.5
	Over 16.5	0	0	5.5	4.5	10.0	0	0	2.0	1.0	3.0
Total	Less than 16	0	0.5	1.5	3.0	5.0	0	0.5	3.0	3.5	7.0
	16 to 16.5	0	1.5	4.0	6.5	12.0	0	1.5	2.0	9.5	13.0
	Over 16.5	0.5	2.5	13.5	8.5	25.0	0.5	3.0	6.5	4.0	14.0
	Grand total	0.5	4.5	19.0	18.0	42.0	0.5	5.0	11.5	17.0	34.0
	Number of persons	1	9	38	37	84	1	10	23	34	68

Note: Percentages are rounded to the nearest 0.5 per cent.

183

TABLE 5-3. SOCIOECONOMIC AREAS OF RESIDENCE OF DROPOUTS AND THEIR CONTROLS (PERCENTAGE DISTRIBUTION)

Socioeconomic Area	Dropouts	Social-Class Controls
1 (high)	1.4	3.0
2	1.4	3.0
3	3.6	5.9
4	11.6	23.8
5	24.6	32.7
6	14.5	7.9
7	34.8	19.8
Rural	5.8	3.9
No info.	2.2	0
Total no.	138	101

TABLE 9-1. SUCCESS OF MARRIAGE RELATED TO SOCIAL CLASS AND INTELLIGENCE OF EARLY-MARRYING GIRLS

Rating of Marriage	Social Class		Intelligence Quartile		Total
	C	D	II	I (low)	
5 (high)	8	2	7	3	10
4	4	5	2	7	9
3	8	2	4	6	10
2	1	4	3	2	5
1	0	8	3	5	8
No info.	0	1	1	0	1
Total	21	22	20	23	43
Mean rating	3.90	2.48	3.37	3.04	3.19

Note: This table presents scores for girls who are members of Class C or D and also below average in intelligence.

TABLE 9-2. SUCCESS OF MARRIAGE RELATED TO PARENTS' MARITAL STATUS (BOYS AND GIRLS)

Parents' Marital Status

Rating of Marriage	Living To-gether	One parent dead	One parent widowed & re-marri'd	Di-vorced or sepa-rated	Di-vorced & re-marri'd	No Infor-mation	Total
5 (high)	30	4	2	5	3	1	45
4	15	3	0	1	3	0	22
3	19	3	2	0	3	0	27
2	6	2	1	4	2	0	15
1	14	5	2	8	5	0	34
Unknown	1	0	1	2	2	0	6
Total	85	17	8	20	18	1	149
Mean rating	3.49	2.94	2.86	2.50	2.81	—	3.20

TABLE 9-3. SOCIAL ADJUSTMENT OF EARLY-MARRYING GIRLS AND BOYS

	Age of Marriage			
	Girls		Boys	
Social-adjustment scores in grades 6, 7, and 9	17 or before	18 or 19	17 or before	18 or 19
Leadership	44.5*	49.9	39.2*	45.8*
Withdrawal	54.0*	50.4	57.0*	50.4
Aggression	51.7	49.3	62.5*	53.9*
Number	53	35	6	32

Note: These are T-scores, with a mean of 50 for the entire age group and a standard deviation of 10. The scores marked by an asterisk are reliably different from the mean of the entire group.

TABLE 12-1. PREDICTION OF INITIAL ADULT ADJUST-
MENT FROM SIXTH, SEVENTH AND NINTH GRADE SCORES
ON LEADERSHIP, AGGRESSION, AND WITHDRAWAL *

Rating on Initial Adult Adjustment	Boys			Girls		
	Le	Ag	Wi	Le	Ag	Wi
5	9	0	1	17	1	1
4	8	0	2	11	1	3
3	1	9	5	5	2	9
2	0	7	5	2	6	9
1	0	10	3	0	4	3
No info.	0	8	2	2	2	5
Total	18	34	18	37	16	30

* This table represents numbers of boys and girls in the high groups in Leadership, Aggression, and Withdrawal. The "high" groups were those in the top 10 per cent (approximate) of the age group, averaged over grades six, seven, and nine.

TABLE 12-2. INITIAL ADULT ADJUSTMENT AND EDUCA-
TIONAL CAREER

Highest Educational Level	Initial Adult Adjustment Rating				
	5	4	3	2	1
College success	48	37	2	0	0
College dropout	0	3	14	1	0
Nursing school or Business college	3	9	2	1	0
High school grad.	7	29	84	27	3
Dropout					
12th grade	1	1	12	8	2
10–11th grade	0	2	30	22	14
7–9th grade	0	0	8	17	18
No info.	0	0	2	2	1
Total	59	82	154	78	38

INDEX

187